The Territory Ahead

Also available from the University of Nebraska Press

Wright Morris: Structures and Artifacts
Photographs 1933–1954

Conversations with Wright Morris (BB 630)
Edited with an introduction by Robert E. Knoll

FOR D. H. LAWRENCE

*"Rip the veil of the old vision across,
and walk through the rent."*

Let me live where I will, on this side is the city, on that the wilderness, and ever I am leaving the city more and more and withdrawing into the wilderness. I should not lay so much stress on this fact if I did not believe that something like this is the prevailing tendency of my countrymen.   HENRY THOREAU

But I reckon I got to light out for the Territory ahead of the rest, because Aunt Sally she's going to adopt and civilize me, and I can't stand it. I been there before.   MARK TWAIN

Wright Morris **THE**

TERRITORY

AHEAD

UNIVERSITY OF NEBRASKA PRESS

LINCOLN/LONDON

Part of the material in Chapters 1, 2, and 14 previously appeared in different form in *The Living Novel: A Symposium*, edited by Granville Hicks, The Macmillan Company, 1957. Excerpts from *The American Scene* by Henry James (copyright 1907 Charles Scribner's Sons) are reprinted with the permission of Charles Scribner's Sons and Alexander R. James. Copyright 1907 by Harper & Bros.; renewal copyright 1935 by Henry James. The Postscript originally appeared in *Partisan Review*, xxviii (1961), 541–551.

UNP

Preface Copyright © 1978 by the University of Nebraska Press
Copyright © 1957, © 1958, © 1961 by Wright Morris
Copyright © 1957 by The Macmillan Company

First Bison Book printing: 1978

Most recent printing indicated by first digit below:
1   2   3   4   5   6   7   8   9   10

Library of Congress Cataloging in Publication Data

Morris, Wright, 1910–
 The territory ahead.

 Reprint of the 1957 ed. published by Harcout, Brace, New York.
 1. American literature—History and criticism. I. Title.
[PS88.M6 1978]   810'.9   77–27989
ISBN 0–8032–3050–8
ISBN 0–8032–8100–5 pbk.

The Bison Book edition, published by arrangement with the author, has been reproduced from the first edition published by Harcourt, Brace and Company, except for the Postscript, which has been reset, and the Preface.

Manufactured in the United States of America

PREFACE TO THE BISON BOOK EDITION

In the twenty years since this book was published, the role of nostalgia in our literature has dwindled as our great expectations have diminished. The backward look, the consuming longing, is no longer a crippling preoccupation of the writer. The national purpose, the national conscience, are currently pressured from other quarters. I am now more inclined to a nostalgic view of nostalgia itself. What a passion it was for those possessed by it! Americans did not invent this torment, but surely we have made the most of its follies, a passion that was crippling to Thomas Wolfe but liberating to the mind of Faulkner. Without a mythic and alluring past American writers of genius, with few exceptions, had little to fuel their imaginations. It gave substance to their dreams of national purpose, and faith to sustain their personal visions. On such evidence the virtues of nostalgia more than compensate for its foibles. It would appear to have generated what was essential to a young nation's boundless and soaring expectations, uninhibited by, and often indifferent to, the obvious.

In one of his letters Keats wrote, "Though a quarrel in the streets is a thing to be hated, the energies displayed in it are fine; the commonest Man shows a grace in his quarrel." This anticipates Hemingway's grace under pressure. Although nostalgia in itself is a disabling obsession, well summed up in Faulkner's "impotent and static rage," the energies displayed through the imagination are both fine and remarkable. It was here, it had had its way with us, and now it is gone. The backward look now in fashion, one that transforms objects into collectibles, and junk into antiques, is not to be confused with the dark fields of Fitzgerald's republic or Huck and Jim adrift on their raft. The mythic past, to the extent we possess it, is the one that exists.

WRIGHT MORRIS

March 1978
Mill Valley, California

CONTENTS

*Real generosity toward the future
lies in giving all to the present.*

ALBERT CAMUS

From Hawthorne to Faulkner the mythic past has generated what is memorable in our literature—but what is not so memorable, what is often crippling, we have conspired to overlook. This is the tendency, long prevailing, to start well then peter out. For the contemporary, both the writer and the reader, this pattern of failure may be more instructive than the singular achievements of the past. The writer's genius, as a rule, is unique, but in his tendency to fail he shares a common tradition. This blight has been the subject of many inquiries, and the prevailing opinion has been that an unresponsive and Philistine culture has, as a rule, corrupted the writer's promise. Such an exception as Henry James, the exile, would merely seem to prove the rule. He succeeded or he failed—depending on the point of view—by becoming a non-American.

"Mr. Henry James, great artist and faithful historian," Joseph Conrad observes, "never attempts the impossible." This would seem to be the opposite, however, of accepted American practice. Failure, not success, is the measure of an artist's achievement. Mr. Faulkner has given this notion fresh currency in a recent statement concerning Thomas Wolfe: Wolfe was the greatest of them all, Faulkner said, because he tried to do the impossible. This is tantamount to saying that the dilettante is superior to the master craftsman, since the master craftsman achieves what he sets out to do. Failure, not achievement, is the hallmark of success. The romantic origins of this statement are less pertinent to this discussion than the prevailing tendency to find in such a statement a profound truth. The great writer *must* fail. In this way we shall know that he is great. In such a writer's failure the public sees a moral victory: what does his failure prove but how sublime and grand the country is? This point of view has so much to recommend it that to call it into question smacks of un-Americanism. It calls, that is, for a shrinking of the national consciousness.

It is the purpose of this book to inquire if this climate of failure is not linked, in a logical fashion, with the prevailing tendency of the American mind to take to the woods. Literally, like Thoreau, or figuratively, like Faulkner, our writers of genius face backward while their countrymen resolutely march forward. It is little wonder, faced with this fact, that we lead such notably schizoid lives.

Reappraisal is repossession, and this book is an act of reappraisal. In such a fashion I seek to make my own what I have inherited as clichés. To make new we must reconstruct, as well as resurrect. The destructive element in this reconstruction is to remove from the object the encrusted cliché. Time itself, in architecture and sculpture, does this in terms of what it leaves us. The fragment means more to us—since it demands more of us—than the whole. The mutilations are what we find the most provocative and beautiful. Since we cannot, in any case, possess the original—which exists in one time and serves one purpose—our reappraisal is an act of re-creation in which the work of art is the raw material. Short of this we are dealing with the bones of a fossil, the remains of a form that has served its purpose.

Such an attitude questions, of course, one of the sentiments most congenial to our nature—the uniqueness and inviolability of art. Art is indeed unique and inviolable—but its uniqueness may lie where we do not choose to look: in the creative response it generates in the participant; in the need he feels to repossess it in his own terms. The creative act itself is self-sufficient, having served the artist's purpose, but it lives on only in those minds with the audacity to transform it. The classic, from such a point of view, is that characteristic statement that finds in each age an echoing response—echoing, but not the same. Hemingway's Huck Finn is not Mark Twain's, nor is my Huck Finn Hemingway's. Nor do I mean to suggest that art itself is atomized in an infinite series of personal impressions—but that it survives, archetypally, in and through an endless series of transformations. Through the Huck Finns, that is—through each age's reappraisal—the young heart is reassured and the consciousness expands.

This book has grown out of an essay written at the suggestion of Granville Hicks, and is an act of synthesis rather than analysis, a personal inquiry in the sense that it grows from my experience as a reader and a writer. No effort has been made to be inclusive, and I do not imply that other evaluations, from other points of view, are not equally useful. This is how it looks to me.

In the nineteenth century the writer took to the woods or the high seas, literally as well as figuratively. In the present century the same flight is achieved through nostalgia, rage, or some such ruling passion from which the idea of the present, the opposing idea, has been excluded. In the American writer of genius the ability to function has been retained—with the exception of James—by depreciating the intelligence.

For more than a century the territory ahead has been the world that lies somewhere behind us, a world that has become, in the last few decades, a nostalgic myth. On the evidence, which is impressive, it is the myth that now cripples the imagination, rather than the dark and brooding immensity of the continent. It is the territory behind that defeats our writers of genius, not America.

Part One

FICTION AND FACT

ONE

TECHNIQUE

AND RAW MATERIAL

"God alive, Sir Knight of the Mournful Countenance," said Sancho, "I cannot bear in patience some of the things that your Grace says! Listening to you, I come to think that all you have told me about deeds of chivalry and winning kingdoms and bestowing islands and other favors and dignities is but wind and lies, all buggery or humbuggery or whatever you choose to call it. For when anyone hears your Grace saying that a barber's basin is Mambrino's helmet, and after four days you still insist that it is, what is he to think except that such a one is out of his mind?"

We have that barber's basin, more crushed and dented than ever, among us today. It symbolizes the state of the imagination in the raw material world of facts. Like Sancho, the modern temper distrusts the processes of the imagination, but it has great faith in the alchemy of the laboratory. High octane and low imagination are the order of the day.

The romantic agony of the poet has been displaced by the agony of the test tube—the compulsive commitments

3

of the poet have given way to the compulsive behavior
of atomic fission. The hallmark of the true agony is that
extinction is preferable to self-examination. The end of
life, public and private, is preferable to the end of the
pursuit of such knowledge.

Technique and raw material are essential to both the
study and the laboratory. By raw material I mean that
comparatively crude ore that has not been processed by
the imagination—what we refer to as *life*, or as experience, in contrast to art. By technique I mean the way that
the artist smelts this material down for human consumption.

A new world, in these terms, will contain more raw
material than an old one. America, that is, is rawer than
Europe. This rawness is comparative, however, since the
brave new world that the explorer discovers contains, on
the whole, only what he comes prepared to find. But a
permissible illusion of rawness exists on each frontier.
And in a nation of expanding frontiers, the illusion of
rawness expands along with them. Technique, in this
pioneer picture, is therefore little more than a clearing
operation—the raw material is the thing, and the technique is a method of collecting it. There usually appears
to be an inexhaustible supply of it. But if you happen
to run out of it where you are, why then you move on to
where it is waiting. It *exists*, that is. It is not something
the artist conjures up.

If the world is a collection of crude barbers' basins which the artist must transmute into gold, both Cervantes and Norman Rockwell, "the most popular, the most loved, of all contemporary artists," give us a lesson in how this trick is done.

"Do you know what I think, Sancho?" said Don Quixote. "I think that this famous piece of that enchanted helmet must by some strange accident have fallen into the hands of someone who did not know, and was incapable of estimating, its worth, and who, seeing that it was of the purest gold and not realizing what he was doing, must have melted down the other half for what he could get for it, while from the remaining portion he fashioned what appears, as you have said, to be a barber's basin."

It is Cervantes who takes us behind the scenes and shows us how the imagination works: we are not merely told that the world is a stage, but how it operates. Technique and raw material are dramatized at the moment that the shaping imagination is aware of itself. We see the way in which the world—in Whitehead's sense—is processed into reality. The transitory, illusive facts are shaped into a fiction of permanence. At the moment that the mind takes the step we think of as characteristically modern, we are taken offstage, into the very wings of the mind itself. We are allowed to see the world, as the raw material, and Don Quixote, the transforming technician. The author, whom we do not see, is the discipline that

turns the Mournful Knight's mad antics to the service of
the heart's desire, the intelligence. Both technique and
raw material—the processed fiction and the raw fact—
confront each other in Don Quixote and Sancho, a legend
of the labyrinthine ways of the imagination itself.

II

The history of fiction, its pursuit of that chimera we
describe as reality, is a series of imaginative triumphs
made possible through technique. In *Mimesis*, Erich
Auerbach has charted this course from Homer to Joyce.
In aesthetic terms, *facts* are those sensations that have
been convincingly processed by the imagination. They are
the materials, the artifacts, so to speak, that we actually
possess.

At the summit of technique we have such a craftsman
as Joyce. There is so little craft in fiction on this scale
that so much craft seems forbidding. Is the end result—
we are inclined to ask ourselves—still alive? Is life, real
or imaginary, meant to be processed as much as that? In
Joyce the dominance of technique over raw material reflects one crisis of the modern imagination. Raw material
has literally dissolved into technique.

In *Finnegans Wake* the world of Dublin happens to be
the raw material that Joyce puts through his process—
but the process, not Dublin, is the thing. It is the process
that will give the raw material its enduring form. A

parallel transformation is still taking place in what we call modern art. In Manet's portrait of Clemenceau the subject has vanished into the method—the method has become painting itself. Both Dublin and Clemenceau are processed into means, rather than ends, since the artist's problem is not to reconstruct the old, but to construct the new. It is characteristic of the mind of Joyce that the city of Dublin, shaped by his ironic craft, should not merely disappear but prove hard to find.

The brave new world has had its share of able craftsmen, but with the exception of Hawthorne and James, both closely linked to the old, they usually lacked what we would call the master touch. Raw material, usually the rawer the better, seemed to be their forte. On certain rare and unpredictable occasions craft might break through this devotion to raw material, but the resulting masterpiece had about it the air of an accident; not so much a crafty man-made thing, as a gift from above. The author usually took pains not to repeat it, or to learn from his experience. *Walden, Leaves of Grass, Moby Dick,* and the *Adventures of Huckleberry Finn* have in common this sense of isolation. Something of a mystery to both the author and the public, they resemble some aspect of a natural force—a pond, a river, a demonic whale—rather than something cleverly contrived by man. They seem to have more in common with Niagara Falls, Mammoth Cave, or Old Faithful than with a particular author, or anything so artificial as art. They are wonders, but *natural* wonders, like the Great Stone Face.

This notion of the natural, the unschooled genius who leaps, like a trout, from some mountain stream, seems to be central to our national egotism. It reappears every day in the child—or the backward, untutored adult— who draws, writes, strums a saw or plays a piano without *ever* having taken a lesson. That lessons might corrupt his talent, and ruin his promise, goes without saying. We believe in doing only what comes naturally.

But those natural moments in which we take so much pride—*Walden, Leaves of Grass, Moby Dick,* and *Huckleberry Finn*—are, without exception, moments of grace under pressure, triumphs of craft. The men who produced them are artists, innovators, of the first magnitude. Each of these statements is a contemporary statement, and each is unique. They represent new levels where, in the words of D. H. Lawrence, the work of art can ". . . inform and lead into new places the flow of our sympathetic consciousness, and it can lead our sympathy away in recoil from things that are dead."

If we now ask ourselves under what pressure these moments of grace are achieved, I believe it is the pressure of the raw material itself. Each of these men felt the need to domesticate a continent. In his essay on Hawthorne, Melville observed: "It is not so much paucity as superabundance of material that seems to incapacitate modern authors."

He had reason to know. It was not lack of material that silenced Herman Melville. The metaphysical woods that he found mirrored in the sea, and which drew him to it, of all aspects of the brave new world were the least inhabited.

III

With the passing of the last natural frontier—that series of horizons dissolving westward—the raw-material myth, based, as it is, on the myth of inexhaustible resources, no longer supplies the artisan with lumps of raw life. All of it has been handled. He now inhabits a world of raw-material clichés. His homemade provincial wares no longer startle and amaze the world. As a writer he must meet, and beat, the old world masters at their own game. In his "Monologue to the Maestro," Hemingway states the problem in his characteristic manner:

There is no use writing anything that has been written better before unless you can beat it. What a writer in our time has to do is write what hasn't been written before or beat dead men at what they have done. The only way he can tell how he is going is to compete with dead men . . . the only people for a serious writer to compete with are the dead that he knows are good. . . .

With this credo the Portrait of the Artist as a Young American is permanently revised. The provincial is out. The dyed-in-the-wool professional is in. Not only do we have to meet the champ, we have to beat him. That calls,

among other things, for knowing who he is. Such a statement could only come from a writer who knows you have
to beat the masters with style and technique, and it is on
these terms that he has won his place in the pantheon.

If raw material is so bad, if it is the pitfall and handicap
to the artist that I am suggesting, why is it that American
writers, through, rather than in spite of, this handicap,
are one of the germinal forces wherever books are read.
Here, I think, we have an instructive paradox. It involves
us in the problem of good and bad taste. Not the good
or bad taste of the artist, but the good or bad taste we
find in his raw material. Good taste—*good* in the sense
that it is fashionable and decorative—usually indicates an
absence of the stuff of life that the artist finds most
congenial. Both the Parthenon and the urban apartment
decorated with Mondrian and Van Gogh resist more than
a passing reference, usually ironic in tone. The over-
processed material, what we sense as overrefinement, is
an almost fatal handicap to the artist: we feel this handicap in James—not in his mind, but in his material—and
it is at a final extremity in Proust. Only a formidable
genius, only a formidable technique, can find in such
material fresh and vital elements.

Bad taste, on the other hand, is invariably an ornament
of vitality, and it is the badness that cries out with meaning, and calls for processing. Raw material and bad taste
—the feeling we have that bad taste indicates *raw* mate-

rial—is part of our persuasion that bad grammar, in both life and literature, reflects *real* life. But bad taste of this sort is hard to find. Bad "good taste" is the world in which we now live.

In reference to Joyce, Harry Levin has said: "The best writing of our contemporaries is not an act of creation, but an act of evocation peculiarly saturated with reminiscences." This observation pertains to Joyce and Proust as it does to Fitzgerald and his dream of Gatsby, or to Hemingway's Nick on "The Big Two-Hearted River." In our time, that is, nostalgia is not peculiarly American.

But the uses to which the past is put allow us to distinguish between the minor and the major craftsman. The minor artist is usually content to indulge in it. But the labyrinthine reminiscence of Proust is conceptual, *consciously* conceptual, in contrast to the highly unconscious reminiscence in *Huckleberry Finn*. Not *knowing* what he was doing, Mark Twain was under no compulsion to do it again.

Twain's preference for *real* life—*Life on the Mississippi*—is the preference Thoreau felt for facts, the facts of Nature, and Whitman's preference for the man-made artifact. Something *real*. Something the hand, as well as the mind, could grasp. Carried to its conclusion this preference begins and ends right where we find it—in autobiography. On this plane raw material and art appear to be identical. *I was there, I saw, and I suffered,* said Whitman, sounding the note, and the preference is still dear to the readers of the *Saturday Evening Post.* Wanting no nonsense, only facts, we make a curious discovery. Facts are like faces. There are millions of them. They are disturbingly alike. It is the imagination that looks behind the face, as well as looks out of it.

Letting the evidence speak for itself, the facts, that is, of the raw-material myth, the indications are that it destroys more than it creates. It has become a dream of abuse rather than use. We are no longer a raw-material reservoir, the marvel and despair of less fortunate cultures, since our only inexhaustible resource at the moment is the cliché. An endless flow of clichés, tirelessly processed for mass-media consumption, now give a sheen of vitality to what is either stillborn or secondhand. The hallmark of these clichés is a processed sentimentality. The extremes of our life, what its contours should be, blur at their point of origin, then disappear into the arms of the Smiling Christ at Forest Lawn. The secretary with the diaphragm in her purse, prepared to meet any emergency, will prove to be a reader of Norman Vincent Peale or Kahlil Gibran. Ten minutes of her luncheon will be turned over to *The Mature Mind.* The raw-material world of facts, of *real* personal life, comes full circle in the unreal phantom who spends real time seeking for his or her self in the how-to-do-it books—How to

Live, How to Love, and, sooner or later, How to Read Books.

What was once raw about American life has now been dealt with so many times that the material we begin with is itself a fiction, one created by Twain, Eliot, or Fitzgerald. *From Here to Eternity* reminds us that young men are still fighting Hemingway's war. After all, it is the one they know best: it was made real and coherent by his imagination.

Many writers of the twenties, that huge season, would appear to be exceptions to the ravages of raw material, and they are. But it is the nature of this exception to prove the rule. In inspiration, the twenties were singularly un-American. An exile named Pound established the standards, and the left bank of Paris dictated the fashions. This lucid moment of grace was Continental in origin. With the exiles' return, however, it came to an end. The craftsmen who shaped and were shaped by this experience—Eliot, Fitzgerald, Crane, Hemingway, and so on—maintained their own devotion to the new standards, but they had little effect on the resurgent raw-material school. Whitman's barbaric yawp, which Pound had hoped to educate, reappeared in the gargantuan bellow of Wolfe and a decade of wrath largely concerned with the seamy side of life.

Once again that gratifying hallucination—the great BIG American novel—appeared in cartons too large for

the publisher's desk. Once again the author needed help
—could one man, singlehanded, tame such a torrent of
life? If the writer caged the monster, shouldn't the editor
teach him to speak? The point was frequently debated;
the editor-collaborator became a part of the creative
project, the mastering of the material as exhausting as
mastering life itself. In a letter to Fitzgerald, who had
suggested that there might be room for a little more
selection, Thomas Wolfe replied: "I may be wrong but
all I can get out of it is that you think I'd be a better
writer if I were an altogether different writer from the
writer I am."

Time and the river—was Fitzgerald suggesting they
reverse themselves? That a writer swim against the very
current of American life? He was, but the suggestion has
never been popular. Tom Wolfe didn't take it, and the
writer who does take it may find himself, however home-
grown, an exile. He swims against the current; and the
farther he swims, the more he swims alone. The best
American fiction is still *escape* fiction—down the river on
a raft, into the hills on a horse, or out of this world on a
ship—the territory ahead lies behind us, safe as the gold
at Fort Knox.

IV

Raw material, an excess of both material and comparatively raw experience, has been the dominant factor in

my own role as a novelist. The thesis I put forward grows out of my experience, and applies to it. Too much crude ore. The hopper of my green and untrained imagination was both nourished and handicapped by it.

Before coming of age—the formative years when the reservoir of raw material was filling—I had led, or rather been led by, half a dozen separate lives. Each life had its own scene, its own milieu; it frequently appeared to have its own beginning and ending, the only connecting tissue being the narrow thread of my *self*. I had been *there*, but that, indeed, explained nothing. In an effort to come to terms with the experience, I processed it in fragments, collecting pieces of the puzzle. In time, a certain over-all pattern *appeared* to be there. But this appearance was essentially a process—an imaginative act of apprehension—rather than a research into the artifacts of my life.

The realization that I had to create coherence, conjure up my synthesis, rather than find it, came to me, as it does to most Americans, disturbingly late. Having sawed out the pieces of my jigsaw puzzle, I was faced with a problem of fitting them together. There is a powerful inclination to leave this chore to someone else. In the work of Malcolm Cowley on William Faulkner, we may have the rudiments of a new procedure. Let the critic do what the author fails to do for himself. As flattering as this concept might be—to both the author and the critic—

it must be clear that the concept is not tenable. The final act of coherence is an imaginative act—not a sympathetic disposal of parts—and the man who created the parts must create the whole into which they fit. It is amusing to think what the mind of Henry James would make of this salvage operation, a surgical redistribution of the parts of a patient who is still alive. Mr. Cowley's service to the reader is important—what I want to put in question is his service to the writer. This is implicit, if unstated, in any piece of reconstruction that attempts to implement what the writer failed to do himself.

This act of piety toward the groping artist—a desire to help him with his raw-material burden—is one with our sentiment that he labors to express the inexpressible. Like a fond parent, we supply the words to his stuttering lips. We share with him, as he shares with us, an instinct that our common burden of experience, given a friendly nudging, will speak for itself. At such a moment the mind generates those evocations peculiar to the American scene: life, raw life of such grace that nature seems to be something brought back alive. Out on his raft Huck Finn muses:

> Two or three days and nights went by: I reckon I might say they swum by, they slid along so quiet and smooth and lovely. Here is the way we put in the time.

In what follows we are putting in our own time. We are there. Memory is processed by emotion in such a way that life itself seems to be preserved in amber. But we know better; we know that it is more than life, and it is this knowledge that makes it so moving—life has been imagined, immortal life, out of thin air. Not merely that boy out on the river, but the nature of the world's imagination, there on the raft with him, will never again be the same. But at the end of his adventures, at the point where the fiction—like the reader—merges into fact, Huck Finn sums it all up in these pregnant words:

But I reckon I got to light out for the Territory ahead of the rest, because Aunt Sally she's going to adopt me and civilize me, and I can't stand it. I been there before.

So has the reader. Aunt Sally has his number, but his heart belongs to the territory ahead.

TWO

THE MYTHIC PAST

If we should now ask ourselves what it is that the common and the uncommon American have in common, the man in the street and the sophisticate, the hillbilly and the Ivy Leaguer, I think we have an answer. Nostalgia. This bond joins, in sweet fraternity, such elements as the *Saturday Evening Post* and the *New Yorker*; such artists as Norman Rockwell and E. B. White. It is the past, the mythic past that is real, in Mr. White's lucid prose and Mr. Rockwell's illustrations. The present exists—in so far as it exists—in order to heighten the comparison. Urban sophisticate and cracker-barrel yokel share the oxygen tent of nostalgia. In their commitments to the past Mr. Rockwell and Mr. White—poles apart in technique—process the same sentiments. It is the past that is real. The second tree from the corner is rooted in it. From this commitment Mr. White distills a memorable blend of truth and poetry, leaving to Mr. Rockwell the less memorable elements. But both craftsmen press the same grapes, and bottle the same vintage. They offer us a sweet or dry version of the past.

Mr. White may be right—no writer states his case with more convincing persuasion—but the rightness or the wrongness of his preference is not central to our discussion. What *goes* in his case is what goes without saying in both the *Saturday Evening Post* and the *New Yorker*. That is nostalgia. An implicit, understandable preference for the past.

But there would seem to be a law that the imagination cannot deal creatively with secondhand material. What has been done has been done. It resists further tampering. There can be only one Hamlet, one Don Quixote, one Ivan Karamazov, and one Huckleberry Finn, although the world, since nature imitates art, will be peopled with their likenesses.

The mind that falls under the spell of such an artist must exorcise this spell before it can be itself. The possession of the reader is the trap for the writer—he must first fall into it, then escape from it. His affection and admiration for the past—above all for the craft that created such a past—must be expressed in an imaginative act that blends both piety and cannibalism. In order to begin anew, as André Malraux has pointed out, the artist must cut the ties that bind him.

Every genius leads a revolt against a previous form of possession . . . it is the fact that he alone, amongst all those whom these works of art delight, should seek, by the same token, to destroy them.

Until he does this he cannot process his own reality. The great tradition is not a pious submission to and maintenance of the *status quo,* but an act of renewal that involves this destructive element.

This goes on—as long as art goes on—before our very eyes. What is currently *raw* in Southern writing derives from the imagination of William Faulkner rather than from the rawness of Southern life itself. This bondage will persist, these *facts* will seem the real ones, until another writer, with his own spell, removes Faulkner's enchantment to replace it with his own.

In a less dramatic way this has occurred to the country at large. The imagination has now left its stamp on all of it. The names on the land now turn up as the themes or the titles of books. The dry places and the wet, the forces natural and unnatural, have been catalogued. Death Valley offers cocktails and innerspring trail rides to the new generation of pioneers, and the words "dude" and "ranch" are now inseparable. Talent now *originates* in Las Vegas, and the same nylon sweaters, with the same walking shorts, are seen on what appear to be the same teen-agers in Red Wing, Minnesota; Nacogdoches, Texas; and the Bronx. The same popular songs, sung by the same singers, are heard in Seneca, Kansas; Winnemucca, Nevada; or in the car cruising along through what is still described as Donner Pass. Of all questions that face the nation, the $64,000 one is uppermost.

The *region*—the region in the sense that once fed the imagination—is now for sale on the shelf with the maple-sugar Kewpies; the hand-loomed ties and hand-sewn moccasins are now available, along with food and fuel, at regular intervals on our turnpikes. The only regions left are those the artists must imagine. They lie beyond the usual forms of salvage. No matter where we go, in America today, we shall find what we just left.

Raw material, the great variety of it, has been the central ornament of American writing since Thoreau went to Walden, and Whitman took to the open road. The vitality of such material is contagious—it alternately charms and appalls the world—but we have come to the end of what is raw in the material vein. Life, raw life, no longer beckons at the edge of the clearing, to be had for the asking, but must be wooed in the parlor with Aunt Sally as chaperone. The impact of a new, raw-material world on a brooding and sympathetic nature, may result, as in the case of Dreiser, in works that seem to lie outside of the realm of technique. In *Sister Carrie*, in *Jennie Gerhardt*, it is not *naturalism* we have, but Dreiser. His virtues can be felt, but not studiously acquired. The apprentice can learn from him little but his faults. Eventually, raw material overwhelms what is native in the native craftsman, since it heaps him with experience only technique will enable him to process.

In Fitzgerald's *The Great Gatsby*, and I think only in *Gatsby*, the mythic vastness of this continent, the huge raw-material banquet that Wolfe bolted, received its baptismal blessing and its imaginative processing:

And as the moon rose higher the inessential houses began to melt away until gradually I became aware of the old island here that flowered for Dutch sailors' eyes—a fresh, green breast of the new world. Its vanished trees, the trees that made way for Gatsby's house, had once pandered in whispers to the last and greatest of all human dreams; for a transitory enchanted moment man must have held his breath in the presence of this continent, compelled into an aesthetic contemplation he neither understood nor desired, face to face for the last time in history with something commensurate to his capacity for wonder.

This is not description, but incantation, an evocation of the dream and our capacity for wonder, which found in the dark fields of the republic its mythic equivalent. Nostalgia, perhaps the most inexhaustible of human sentiments, found in this green world of the imagination its permanent refuge, out of time, out of reach, but not out of mind.

II

"Try to be one of the people," Henry James advised the writer, "on whom nothing is lost!" and it was his

ironic fate, in being such an artist, to alienate himself
from the American reader, on whom his formidable
craftsmanship is all but lost. It is neither through subject
matter nor taste, but through sheer brilliance of technique
that James is exiled from his countrymen. He transformed our raw material to the point where we found
it unrecognizable.

In American experience, raw material and nostalgia
appear to be different sides of the same coin. The rawer
the material, the more nostalgia it evokes—rawness being
the hallmark of the real thing, the natural. The classic
examples of nostalgia, however, prove to be triumphs of
technique: Huckleberry Finn is such a triumph over Tom
Sawyer, just as Faulkner is a triumph over Wolfe. And
yet the tension that exists between the artist and his material—between the imaginary past and the raw-material
present—appears to generate what is fresh and distinguished in our writing, from *Winesburg, Ohio*, to *The
Adventures of Augie March*.

Privately, in the depths of our being, we are Huckleberry Finns fleeing from Aunt Sally. Publicly we create
and promote the very civilization we privately reject. With
our eyes fixed on the past we walk, blindfolded, into
the future. It is little wonder the American mind sometimes wonders where it is going, and what, indeed, it
is to be an American. On the evidence we might say an
American is a man who attempts to face both ways. In the

eyes of the world we are the future, but in our own eyes we are the past. Nostalgia rules our hearts while a rhetoric of progress rules our words.

A free man must be free to live where he must, admitting to the compulsions of his nature, in the woods with Thoreau, on a raft with Huck Finn, or sauntering down the Open Road with Whitman. But we forget that Thoreau, a Yankee realist to the marrow, after two years in the woods called off the experiment. Thoreau called it off, but we prefer to think that he is permanently anchored at Walden Pond. That is where his life, as well as his experiment, seems to end for us. His own prevailing tendency was modified by the woody grain of his experience, but in the minds of his countrymen it is still the tendency that remains.

Stock taking, inventory, is the first effort of the mind to make itself at home. We see it in Thoreau—it took him to Walden for both a personal and a Nature stock taking—we see it in the Homeric catalogue and poetic inventory of Whitman. But how does one do it where the home will not stay *put?* Where the stock of items on the shelves changes every day? Whitman did not feel this burden as we do—not until his later years—but he began under an even greater handicap. There was simply too much. The mind staggered under the weight of it. The impulse to get away from it all—as trifling as it may now seem to us—sent Thoreau to Walden and

Whitman out on the Open Road. The pattern, however embryonic, is being set up. It is a pattern of flight from a world that will not stand still. The rising tide of cities, and of men, not to mention the appalling flood of objects, forces the man who is aware of these objects into a retreat. It is why we see Tom Wolfe, like a berserk Paul Bunyan, trying to gulp one world and plow under another. It is also why exile has for the American artist a peculiar charm. Somewhere—somewhere *else*, that is—perhaps the world stands still. Perhaps there he can put his thoughts in order—if he has any. But it is raw material that puts him to flight, and as a rule, like Huck Finn, he slips the noose of Aunt Sally and makes for the territory ahead. That is usually where we find him—if we take the trouble to look for him. Huck Finn is still out on the river, on his raft, drifting through the landscape currently leased to Mr. William Faulkner, but otherwise unchanged. The same natives and Indians still peer at him from the scrub along the shore. The same virtues are being defended, the same changes are being deplored, and the same fears of the future send refugees into the past.

III

In a review of Wolfe's *Letters*, Malcolm Cowley observed: "Considering his dependence on what he remembered, Wolfe was lucky that his adolescence, with its intense perceptions, lasted much longer than it does with most writers."

Writer and critic, in this observation, are in common agreement as to what counts. What counts is adolescence, with its intense perceptions, and Wolfe was luckier than most since his adolescence lasted the length of his life. His greatest piece of luck, that is, was that he never grew up. He was Huckleberry Finn Wolfe, out on one raft or another, carried along by Time and the River toward that never-never land of heart's desire, the territory ahead. He got away from Aunt Sally by growing bigger, but without growing *up*. The dream of adolescence is the giant who remains a boy at heart.

Something in American sentiment and sensibility prefers it that way. We want our raw material raw. We often want it rawer than it actually is. On a practical, day-by-day level this is the preference we have for the man who *feels*, and the distrust we feel for the man who *thinks*. It is the root and the flower of the anti-egghead platform in American life. The thinking man, above all the artist whose art transforms a sow's ear into a silk purse, is understandably the enemy of the man who prefers the sow's ear. Anti-eggheadism is not a simple, semiliterate prejudice. It is rooted in a central American presumption that life, raw life, and material, raw material, is superior to the form, the abstraction, that the mind must make of it. The raw material we can get our hands on, the *form* eludes our grasp. Here is where science, applied science, with its conversion of the crude into something refined, something useless into something useful, deeply satisfies the American instinct for the artifact. It is the nature of art to be immaterial, the conceptual act must be grasped by the mind: what appears to be solid is transformed into a vapor thinner than air. That, indeed, is its very indestructibility. Aspirin and barbiturates are factual things, they kill real pain and promote real sleep, but the pain and the lack of sleep arise from invisible fears. Only the laying on of invisible hands will quiet them.

The principle of waste, on which so much of our life and economy seems grounded, is not one that pays off imaginatively. These losses prove to be irreparable. The isolated monuments, the isolated efforts, that characterize the American imagination, symbolize the isolation in which Americans live. Connections are missing. The whole does not add up to something more than the sum of the parts. No synthesizing act of the imagination has as yet transformed us into a nation. We come by our nature *naturally*. We are joined by highways, networks, and slogans, not by imaginative acts. Mother's Day, Father's Day, and Thanksgiving now join us in a bond of ready-made greetings, double-breasted turkeys, and the queues that form where unwanted holiday gifts are exchanged. The Everyman in America will soon be the one who has Everything.

How did we get this way? By doing—as the song says—what comes naturally. What comes naturally, that is, to us. Mark Twain's preference for life, *real* life, in contrast to the life in fiction of Huck Finn, he makes clear in a letter to an unidentified correspondent:

Now then: as the most valuable capital, or culture, or education usable in the building of novels is personal experience, I ought to be well equipped for that trade. I surely have the equipment, a wide culture and all of it real, none of it artificial, for I don't know anything about books.

He knew quite a bit about books, of course, but the nature of the boast is instructive. He felt it was better that he shouldn't. That he had gone to no school but the school of hard knocks. He persuaded himself to believe— in spite of knowing better—that in the building of novels the only equipment a man needed was personal experience, preferably lots of it.

Now personal experience, especially too much of it, actually constitutes an obstacle to the craft of fiction. Too much raw material is as great a hazard as not enough. The hopper of the shaping imagination cannot process too great a load of personal experience. Every publishing season, if not several times a season, we bear witness to this fact. Huge slabs of raw life, the rawer the better, are offered to us. The figure of Tom Wolfe bolting, in his hunger, more than he could swallow without choking symbolizes this dilemma but has done little to diminish it. The truth is, the spectacle exhilarates us. Out of Texas a few years ago—and from where else but from out of Texas?—came what was modestly described as the biggest novel in the world. Naturally. There was hardly a ripple of surprise. When one reflects that Texas, tremendous as it is, is still only a part of the United States, the problem that faces the American novelist is staggering. Life—all of our lives, that is—is just too big and grand a thing to pin down in a book. It would take a giant to do it—and several giants have tried. One from Minnesota, almost seven feet tall, gave it a try until the public lost interest, and we all know Tom Wolfe's huge grapple with the continent. We all knew—even as Wolfe did—that he would fail. He had to fail in order to prove how BIG we were. He had to fail, since what he set himself to do was impossible. Just the other day, William Faulkner, in one of his now-frequent interviews, referred to Thomas Wolfe as the greatest American of them all.

Why? Because he tried to do the impossible. The romantic agony could hardly be better phrased, nor failure made so credible and flattering. To fail, that is, is the true hallmark of success.

Coming from Mr. Faulkner this judgment reveals, in all its lush natural disorder, the schizoid soul of the creative American. It tells us more of Mr. Faulkner than meets the eye in his works. Wolfe's verbal bacchanal, a Walpurgisnacht of infinite adolescent yearning and seminal flow, left in its wake a ruin of rhetoric dear to the American heart. A sentimental scene of havoc testifying to the powers of raw American life. In Tom Wolfe was reborn the myth of the native force that would brook no restraint, and we have not yet cleared away the alluvial deposit of his rhetoric. The love that has no appeasement, the quest that has no resolution, the hunger that has no gratification is highly recommended as suitable fare for growing minds. Wolfe's "insatiable appetite for life" is put forward as part of his genius rather than as a disturbing and pitiless form of his impotence. It is in Wolfe's recently published letters that we find the key to his power as a writer. He is an author of confessions—romantic confessions in the manner of Rousseau—and when he is free of the demands of fiction, the problems of creation, he is free to tell us *all*, which is precisely what he does. His chronic incapacity for selection—in confessions *everything* matters—may soon relegate the letters to the limbo of the fiction; but as a writer of confessions his gifts and his torments were in balance. All he had to do, all he wanted to do, was tell us how he *felt*, and in this he succeeded.

But Wolfe's great public success is a measure of the public need. He can best be understood as a martyr to the American greed for life. What we observe in Wolfe is a man eating: a man whose eating does him no good. His books offer us the spectacle of the artist as a cannibal. Life, both literature and life, was something he wanted to devour. How possess, how truly possess, the visible? Wolfe fled this impasse like a man pursued by the hound of heaven; his personal solution was to keep moving, tirelessly tramping up and down the gangplanks of the world. His artistic solution was to write the same book over and over again. Each time in the hope that his self-doubt would stop tormenting him. The one intuition that did not betray him was his haunting sense of artistic failure. The world-wide chorus of praise did not beguile him. He *knew*. As a martyr to our greed, our lust for life that makes life itself an anticlimax, he is such proof as we need that appetite and raw material are not enough.

I have singled out Wolfe because he symbolizes, in his life and in his art, certain native traits, virtues we would call them, carried to the point of self-destruction. An insatiable hunger, an insatiable desire, is not the sign of life but of impotence. Impotence, indeed, is part of the romantic agony. If one desires what one cannot have, if one must do only what cannot be done, the agony in the garden is of self-induced helplessness. It is Wolfe's tragic distinction that he suffered this agony for all of us.

IV

If William Faulkner has become, as there is some reason to believe, a victim of his own transfiguring imagination, he now inhabits a world that is more enduring than the one he left. This new world is compounded, as the old was not, of indestructible elements. Like Henry James, through sheer brilliance of technique Faulkner has transformed his raw material to a point where most of us find it unrecognizable. This shocks us, but we are never led to doubt—as we are with James—that the raw material is still there, since it is the nature of Faulkner's transformation to heighten its apparent *rawness*. It is precisely the rawness of it that has amazed the world. It justifies the conception, derived from our fiction, of a wilderness as yet untamed, a violent land where such goings-on are commonplace. It is also apparent that Faulkner is a stylist, but to admit that this world is a product of "technique" would be to say that his books are not *echt* American—not representative, that is, of our eruptive, volcanic life. So they read him as we do, because he is raw, but the spell he has thrown on the world's imagination is a real spell; and, like all real spells, it is pure technique. In his madness, that is, there is method. Here it is at work in *Absalom, Absalom!*

There was a wistaria vine blooming for the second time that summer on a wooden trellis before one window, into which sparrows came now and then in random gusts, making a dry vivid dusty sound before going away: and opposite Quentin, Miss Coldfield in the eternal black which she had worn for forty-three years now, whether for sister, father or nothusband none knew, sitting so bolt upright in the straight hard chair that was so

tall for her that her legs hung straight and rigid as if she had
iron shinbones and ankles, clear of the floor with that air of impotent and static rage like children's feet, and talking in that
grim haggard amazed voice until at last listening would renege
and hearing-sense self-confound and the long-dead object of her
impotent yet indomitable frustration would appear, as though by
outraged recapitulation evoked, quiet inattentive and harmless,
out of the biding and dreamy and victorious dust.

This outrage of language, this squeezing on of color,
is intended to produce a specific effect. This effect is
transformation. The raw material, strictly speaking, has
disappeared. It is hard to overpraise the charge and revelation this passage carries. Here is the mind of Faulkner's
South, an old shell buried in the earth, but one has the
feeling that it is about to go off. The heat and summer
stillness, the random gusts of sparrows, and Miss Coldfield in her eternal black, all contribute to a scene that
totters on the edge of violence. Through Faulkner the
mind of the South finds its expression—if not its deliv-
erance. But neither rage nor outraged recapitulation will
revive the long-dead dream of the past, and out of the
dreamy victorious dust conjure up for us a convincing
present.

v

When Faulkner tells us that men are indestructible, we
are, being men, reassured to hear it, but if we live and

have our being in our time we know that this is not so. The destructive element is inherent in man's very will to create. In atomic fission this fact breaks through the pious clichés associated with creation—any creation—to reveal the risks involved in any truly creative act. In the act, that is, of making anything new. A rhetorical passage will neither redeem man nor save him from himself.

Since coming out of retirement, William Faulkner less and less resembles citizen Faulkner, of Oxford, Mississippi, and more and more one of the characters in his books. He invites us to regard him, pen in hand, at the open door of a New Orleans brothel, advising the young writer that the house of ill fame affords ideal conditions for creative work.

This is the voice of a past no longer of use to us. It speaks out again, with echoing remoteness, in and between the lines of his Nobel Prize statement. "I believe that man will not merely endure," he tells us, "he will prevail." These words generate more heat than light. Such light as they do generate illuminates a scene that is far from reassuring, with author Faulkner surrounded by a curious assortment of bedfellows. Thousands who would not, or could not, read his books find this statement of faith wonderfully fortifying. In their minds it amounts to a rejection of his truly creative work. The appeal of the statement seems to lie in the hope that Mr. Faulkner, once a rebel of sorts, has at long last seen the light and returned to the fold, admitting that he believes what we all had the good sense to believe all along.

More convincingly, it seems to me, Mr. Faulkner also spoke of our fear of annihilation, but I believe it is survival—the *wrong* kind of survival—that haunts the mind of the artist. It is not fear of the bomb that paralyzes his will—a fear, that is, that man has no future—but, rather, a disquieting and numbing apprehension that such future as man has may dispense with art. With *man*, that is, such as we now know him, and such, for all his defects, as art has made him. It is the *nature* of the future, not its extinction, that produces in the artist such foreboding, the prescient chill of heart of a world without consciousness.

This unconscious world grows, all too palpably, out of the manifold tendencies that prevail around him, and the habit of science, applied science, to dispense with the need of art. The artist does not want man merely to prevail, but to prevail as he has been able to conceive him. A more fully conscious, fully sentient being, rather than a less. The survival of men who are strangers to the nature of this conception is a more appalling thought than the extinction of the species. This seeming paradox is at the core of the mind's anxiety. Nor is the survival of such men a fiction, but exists in fact in those men whose brains, as we say, have been washed, or whose tensions have been relieved by the drug or the surgical knife.

Part Two

THE STATE OF NATURE

THREE

TO THE WOODS

HENRY THOREAU

I went to the woods because I wished to live deliberately, to front only the essential facts of life, and see if I could not learn what it had to teach, and not, when I came to die, discover that I had not lived.

This statement, by one of the world's free men, has captivated and enslaved millions. It is a classic utterance, made with such art that what is not said seems nonexistent, civilization and its ways a mere web of *in*essentials, distracting man from the essential facts of life. The texture of this language and the grain of this thought are one and the same. To fall under its spell is to be in possession of *one* essential self. A sympathetic mind may find the call irresistible. The essential facts of life will seem to be these facts, all others but stratagems, snares, and delusions, although the facts to support such a conclusion are not self-evident. They are implied, but implied with such persuasion they seem facts. That is Thoreau's intention. But his art is greater than his argument. Although he sought to persuade through *facts*,

through the testimony of the raw material, it is his craft
as a writer that gives his facts conviction, and his example
such power. It is his art, not his facts, that sent his readers
to the woods.

As André Malraux points out in *The Creative Act,*
the artist is launched on his career not by the supremely
beautiful face, but by the supremely beautiful painting.
It is not just the Woods, but *Thoreau's Woods,* that cap-
tivate us. What he chooses to give us is so patently essential—to the picture he is painting—and what he withholds
is so plainly inessential, we feel, to life. It is all a matter
of selection. Of art, that is.

The American mind, the Yankee imagination, had sap
and substance before this man spoke, but I believe we can
say it had no grain until Thoreau. It is the natural grain
of this mind that still shapes our own. The self-induced
captivity of the American mind to some concept of Nature
—NATURE writ large—can be traced, it would seem,
to the shores of Walden Pond. Here is the first contour
map of what we might call our *natural* state of mind.

With his customary intuition concerning things American, D. H. Lawrence, in his *Studies in Classical American
Literature,* points this out.

NATURE.
I wish I could write it larger than that.
N A T U R E.
Benjamin [Franklin] overlooked NATURE. But the French

Crèvecœur spotted it long before Thoreau and Emerson worked
it up. Absolutely the safest thing to get your emotional reactions
over is NATURE.

The unmistakable accuracy of this barb makes us wince.
Nature—even Nature tooth and claw—is child's play
when confronted with *human* nature. The problem, reduced to its essentials, is NATURE v. Human Nature.
It was this problem that led Thoreau to take to the
woods. But he would not have been led there—he more
or less tells us—if he had not believed that taking to the
woods was the prevailing tendency of his countrymen.

In *Walden* that prevailing tendency received its classical form. Back to Nature was not new with Thoreau—
it had, in fact, lost the gloss Crèvecoeur gave it—but
Thoreau endowed it with a civilized respectability. The
romantic wash of color is replaced with the essential facts.
But the result—since he was an artist—was to heighten
the romantic effect. Through the sharp eyes of this capital
realist, NATURE, writ large, looked even more inviting, and the realistic myth took precedence over the
romantic one. It remains, to this day, a characteristic
quality of the American wilderness.

Flight from something, we can say without quibbling,
was foreign to Thoreau's mind, and we know that when
he turned his back on the city it was *toward* the facts—
not away from them. In his own mind he was facing the

very facts that his friends and neighbors turned away
from, and it is this sentiment, not a romanticized Nature,
that gives *Walden* its power. But in a culture of cities,
as the country was then becoming, this sentiment went
against the very grain of culture, and became, in time,
a deliberate rejection of the essential facts of this culture.

In 1845, when Thoreau went to Walden, he had a
continental wilderness lying *before* him, and he was
hardly in a position to see that he had actually turned
his back on the future. Or that the prevailing tendency
of Americans was *flight*. Flight, not from what they had
found, but from what they had created—the very culture
of cities they had labored to establish.

Each of these cultural centers, each of these established
towns, became a fragment of Europe and a past to get
away from—the prevailing tendency of Americans being
what it was. Thoreau did not expose this tendency to
examination—he accepted it. It satisfied, after all, the
drift and grain of his own mind. He *began* at that point—
in a language and a tone similar to that which informed
the Declaration of Independence. He established, as that
document sought to, certain inalienable human rights.
One of them being to take to the woods, if and when you
felt the need.

The principle of turning one's back on unpleasant facts
—unpleasant because they were so deeply inessential, so
foreign, in a way, to our essential Nature—is one *nat-*

urally congenial to the American mind. Thoreau gave this principle its classic utterance. In his spirit, if not in his name, we still take to such woods as we can find. If his genius had been of another kind he might have scrutinized this principle, rather than Nature, but it was his destiny to be the archetypal American. To put, that is, the prevailing tendency to a rigorous test. That he did; that he did and found it wanting, since he both went to the woods and then left them, is an instructive example of how a necessary myth will survive the conflicting facts. The wilderness is now gone, a culture of cities now surrounds us, but the prevailing tendency of Thoreau's countrymen—his more gifted countrymen—is still to withdraw into a private wilderness. William Faulkner is the latest, but he will not be the last, to pitch his wigwam in the pine-scented woods.

If other American classics have been more widely read —and as a rule they would be children's classics—none has left such an impression where it counts the most: on impressionable men. In Thoreau they see the archetypal *man* as well as the American. He is our first provincial with this universal mind. Under the spell of his style his raw material, that little piece of it around Walden Pond, was processed into a universal fact. There it stands, like an act of Nature, having little to do with the man who made it, and, as so often happens, we henceforth have little to do with him. He walks off—he seems to pass like the seasons—leaving us with his pond. With all those facts, essential and inessential, gleaming like a scimitar in the sun, not to mention the problems that his stay in the woods did not resolve.

We have his word for it that Walden was not enough. Is another life of quiet, *very* quiet, desperation all that lies in store? The rest is silence. There is nothing for us to do but go to Walden and see for ourselves.

Somewhere between Walden Pond and Boston—at some point of tension, where these dreams cross—the schizoid soul of the American is polarized. On the one hand we are builders of bridges and cities, we are makers of things and believers in the future. On the other we have a powerful, *private* urge to take to the woods, as we so often do. Sometimes a note left on the bureau, or one tucked into the vest, asks those who still love us to please forgive us, and it usually goes without saying that those who truly love us will understand. After all, it is still the prevailing tendency. To the woods, if we can find them; if we *can't*, then, to the dogs.

It is in the woods at Walden that the shape of things to come is formulated. Here the American mind is divided down its center, fact against fact. At the threshold of our literature the prevailing tendency is given its classic statement and justification. Turn your back on the city, the civilized inessential, and withdraw into the wilderness. Turn your back on those things built with hands, and withdraw into a world not made with hands. The territory ahead lies behind you. *Allons donc!* Take to the woods.

What we have is Nature, NATURE writ large. But it was Thoreau who was the first to remind us that men lead lives of quiet desperation, and another year at Walden, we have reason to believe, he would have been leading one of them. But after two years he had had it. He left the woods, he tells us, for as good a reason as he went there. We have to take that on credit, however, since he does not tell us how it worked out. There is no equally reassuring volume on the world he went back to. Walden was an experiment, he says, and what he learned from it was this: that if a man advances confidently in the direction of his dreams, and endeavors to actually live the life he has imagined, he will meet with a success unexpected in the common hours.

To that we can say *Good!* So he says, and so we believe. But in what direction, pray, now led his dreams? We know only that they led him into the wilderness, not out of it. He does not trouble to tell us in what way his prevailing tendency reversed itself, or, if it did not, how and why it lost its efficacy. No other tendency, of equal inspiration, took its place. Having entered upon and completed his experiment, Thoreau then took eight years to formulate his report, and it stands as the central experiment of his life. And yet we know he went on living. We even know he went on writing. But neither his living nor his writing found another center, another *tendency*, that engaged him like the one that took him to the woods. We might say that having finished with that experiment, he had finished with his life. There is more day to dawn, he reassures us, but he is silent on what day it might be, and in our hearts we feel that the man we know is still in the woods.

What *kind* of man was he? Any number of men, most of them distinguished, have added their touches to his self-portrait. They reaffirm, rather than rearrange, the classical lines. Emerson likened the taking of his arm to the taking of a piece of wood. It would be sound, grainy wood. The elbow honed and polished like the handle of a cane.

But in the main the self-portrait is more than enough. He would ask us to face him as he himself sought to face the facts.

If you stand right fronting and face to face to a fact, you will see the sun glimmer on both its surfaces, as if it were a cimiter, and feel its sweet edge dividing you through the heart and marrow, and so you will happily conclude your mortal career. Be it life or death, we crave only reality. If we are really dying, let us hear the rattle in our throat and feel the cold in the extremities; if we are alive, let us go about our business.

What business? Ah, there's the rub. Not any ordinary business, certainly, since he has just told you, in no uncertain terms, that in nine chances out of ten your *business* is killing you off. It is why you are dying. It is why, as you read him, he has the ring of truth. It is why the essential facts seem to be that we must go to the woods ourselves if we are to live deep and suck the marrow out of life. It is our busy-ness—if we want to face the facts— that is killing us.

This unexamined paradox is one of many that Thoreau leaves with the reader—forever leaves with him, that is, since a volume on that subject never appeared. *Walden,* like *Huckleberry Finn,* is a *beginning*—the opening chapter of a life, a story, one that enthralls us, but with all the remaining chapters missing.

A capital realist, the archetypal honest man, when Thoreau had had enough of the woods he left them— but the facts of his life among men are neither essential nor reassuring. What *could* follow on such a beginning? Deep in our hearts we know that the best has been lived, that we have now had it, which is why we don't ask, why we will settle for a pond, a raft, and Huck Finn.

Behind all this talk about facts, and fine talk it is, one fact escapes comment. There is no other business; no other essential business. One leaves the pond to disappear, like an echo, into the wings. The curtain comes down. The lights come on. Can that be the end? It can't—but those are all the facts we are going to get. In the begin- ning, and a very unforgettable beginning it was, a man went deliberately into the woods. We know that for a fact. But there is very little evidence, of the same order, that he ever came out.

I should not talk about myself so much [he tells us] if there were anybody else whom I knew as well. Unfortunately I am confined to this by the narrowness of my experience.

The revelation of this statement may lead us to overlook its accuracy. The narrowness of his experience is one of the essential facts in his book. I am not concerned with the absence of those things that we now exploit. On such matters as women and sex we can respect his silence. What he chooses to tell us is much more to the point. The insights of Freud—imaginative in nature—have made it difficult, if not impossible, to face the facts of an age different from our own. I would like to suggest that the myth of Nature—writ large, as Thoreau wrote it—can be as overwhelming, traumatic in fact, as the myth of Sex. It is the myth of Nature that concerns us in Thoreau. He turned to Nature as D. H. Lawrence *turned* to Sex, and both transformed what they saw, what they found, to suit the needs of their genius and their temperament. It is difficult to say which offers the greater handicap. Each man sees, in the mirror of his choice, what he is compelled to see. For all of the material details, the counting of nails and beans, Walden Pond is a mythic, personal vision, and in its depths lurk such

facts as it is the genius of the beholder to see. It is on the
same map, and no other, as Huck Finn's mighty river,
and its memorable facts are the product of the same
chemistry, the poet's imagination processing the raw-
material facts.

If we now ask Thoreau about his own *business,* he will
give us a curious answer. His true profession was, he
would have us know, a "saunterer." If this word has a
strong romantic coloration—we *see* Thoreau in the
woods, but we do not see him saunter—it is still consistent with his role in the myth. The busy man has no time
to saunter. In fact, he has no place. One saunters in
Nature, plucking a leaf, chewing a twig. It is the saunterer who stops and asks in amazement, "What is the
grass?" It is the saunterer who has the time to tell you
that it is the flag of his disposition, or better yet, the
beautiful uncut hair of the graves. It is the saunterer who
leans and loafs at his ease. And with that picture, that
telling self-portrait, we know, in our bones, that Thoreau
was no saunterer. We know only, thanks to his statement, that he wanted to be. But I believe it no accident,
however, that the archetypal saunterer of our dreams,
like the archetypal Nature man, Thoreau, began precisely at the point where Thoreau left off. The prevailing
tendency, having finished with Thoreau, reappears as a
sauntering Song in Walt Whitman, as he makes his way,
idly, down the endlessly open road. Walt Whitman, a

Kosmos, of Manhattan the son, is that other half of the
Nature picture, but this time it is Human Nature—and
Walt Whitman's own. Turbulent, fleshy, sensual, eating,
drinking, and breeding, Walt Whitman wants space, he
wants air, he wants OUT!

Unscrew the locks from the doors!
Unscrew the doors themselves from the jambs!

In theory, if not in practice, in private, if not in public,
this was, and still is, the prevailing tendency of his
countrymen.

FOUR

THE OPEN ROAD

WALT WHITMAN

> Our inability to place the man, intellectually, and find a type
> and a reason for his intellectual state, comes from this: that the
> revolt he represents is not an intellectual revolt. Ideas are not at
> the bottom of it. It is a revolt from drudgery. It is the revolt of
> laziness.   —John Jay Chapman

The word "saunterer," ill suited to Thoreau, slips onto
the relaxed figure of Whitman like a glove. It suits him,
but it would look a little strange on most of us. "Saunterer" is not a word that the language has made its own.
We understand the word, in our fashion, but we would
not be at ease with the type. We have another word for
the man with the grass-stained knees, usually seen in the
park, loafing at his ease on a bench, or stretched his length
on the lawn while he observes a spear of summer grass.
We have both another word, and we make two distinc-
tions. In our busy world he is the man without a business.
The good, familiar, not quite respectable, word for this
man is "tramp." It is a word that would have made

Thoreau bridle, but we can feel, with affectionate assurance, that Walt Whitman would have worn it the way he wore his hat—with an air, an air of assurance that all *free* men are tramps at heart. They have been in chains, but Walt Whitman will set them free.

Afoot and light-hearted I take to the open road
Healthy, free, the world before me,
The long brown path before me leading wherever I choose.

It is left to Whitman, the democrat en masse, to spell out what Thoreau glossed over, to yawp out over the roofs what a respectable Yankee would keep to himself.

Allons! whoever you are come travel with me
Traveling with me you find what never tires.

And to Thoreau's grainy challenge—"If we are living, let us go about our business!"—genial, gregarious, affectionate Walt Whitman would smile. Like a big friendly dog, he would tolerantly wag his head. If we are really living, he would tell us, we will go about *no* business. If we are living, we will take to the open road and live.

Allons! the road is before us. . . .
Let the tools remain in the workshop! let the money remain unearned!
Let the school stand. Mind not the cry of the teacher.
Let the preacher preach in the pulpit! Let the lawyer plead in the court, and the judge expound the law.

Such stuff would wither the soul of Thoreau, and yet
Walt Whitman is his child, his devoted offspring. It is
Whitman who carries to its conclusion Thoreau's admirable beginning. It is Whitman who *lives* the prevailing
tendency.

I tramp a perpetual journey, (come listen all)
My signs are a rain-proof coat, good shoes, and a staff cut from
    the woods,
No friend of mine takes his ease in my chair,
I have no chair, no church, no philosophy,
I lead no man to a dinner table, library, exchange,
But each man and each woman of you I lead upon a knoll,
My left hand hooking you round the waist,
My right hand pointing to landscapes of continents and the
    public road.

With his usual accuracy, Thoreau described his romance with Walden as an experiment—it is the safe
Yankee testing the ice to see if it will bear the load.
Whitman does not test or experiment. At the risk of
exclusion, that is, he does not discriminate. All roads lie
open, all friends are good friends, and all journeys perpetual. As Thoreau is the archetypal honest man, the
square peg in the world's round holes, Whitman is the
archetype that lurks even deeper—the professional
tramp. The man whose business is no business, whose roof
is the sky, whose house is the road, and whose law is the
law of comrades.

Camerado, I give you my hand
I give you my love more precise than money,
I give you myself before preaching or law.
Will you give me yourself? Will you come travel with me?
Shall we stick by each other as long as we live?

As this voice stops speaking one can almost see Camerado Thoreau recoil, with Yankee reserve, and with Yankee reason. As long as one lives can be a long time. He may not *want* a love more precise than money. He may not *want* yourself before preaching or law. And as for sticking by each other as long as you live, nothing would send Camerado Thoreau back to the woods any faster. And it might keep him there.

Thoreau might risk the *experiment* of friendship, but he would flee like the plague the *movement* of brotherhood. And it is a movement, not an experiment, that Whitman sings. He carries a banner, and like the Pied Piper he plays a tune. He does not, that is, take either to the woods or the road alone.

Camerado! he chants, throwing wide his arms, give me your hand: and it is such an offer, it is fear of such an offer, that continues to make Walden Pond so attractive. At Walden one is free of complications of just that sort: human complications, emotional complications. Absolutely the safest thing to get your emotional reactions over is NATURE, said Lawrence. But Whitman rushes in where Thoreau hesitates to tread. He literally takes to the open road looking for it. For what? For camerados. It is not what one finds in the woods. The woods are where, whittling very slowly, a man might carve out a friend, or see him honed down by Nature. The road is where one finds a camerado like oneself. A wanderer, perhaps, who seeks a companion like oneself.

Shoulder your duds, dear son, and I will mine, and let us hasten
  forth,
Wonderful cities and free nations we shall fetch as we go.

Having given sanction, if not birth to such a child, Thoreau would have been horrified to see it in operation. He did not mean, he would tell us, that such a tendency as *that* should prevail. The men he visualized were men like himself, men who went *privately* about their business. Walt Whitman's business is in public—whether the public is there or not. If they are not there—if, that is, you Camerado, are not there with him—he will report how it was *as if* you were there. Having gone to take a sun bath Whitman reports:

So hanging clothes on rail near by, keeping old broadbrim straw on head and easy shoes on feet, haven't I had a good time the last two hours!

We can see him. Easy shoes on feet, broadbrim straw on head, the sweet, easy sanity of the picture beguiles us. The old man, his clothes on a rail, in comradely harmony with Nature—is open to all in the way that Walden is curiously private. The *open* air, the *open* road, the *open* arms, the *open* mind, are at the opposite pole from Thoreau's instinct for privacy. Whitman feels the need, his clothes hanging on the rail, to have you, Camerado, there beside him, *your* clothes on the rail, in an open-air fellowship of minds and bodies. The cult of Nudism, we can be sure, would have appealed to him. Almost single-handedly he returned to the body the bodiless transcendent soul of Emerson and Thoreau, and to the wisdom of the body he gave instinctive preference.

I believe in the flesh and the appetites,
Seeing, hearing, feeling are miracles, and each part and tag of
    me is a miracle.
Divine am I inside and out, and I make holy whatever I touch
    or am touch'd from,
The scent of these armpits aroma finer than prayer,
This head more than churches, bibles, and all the creeds.

It is the body that sings in the Song of Myself, and as that song dies, as it fades, that is, into garrulity, the Song as song becomes incidental. It is the body that remains. *One* body to be exact, that of Walt Whitman, he whose clothes were left hanging on the rail, and on whose bones, as he tells us, there grows no sweeter fat. "The Song of Myself," imperceptibly, becomes the cult of his personality—the good gray poet who looks out at us from so many photographs. But that is at the end of the road; back at the beginning is a world of things,

Homeric in range and freshness, as they were at the Greek morning of the world. Like Homer, Walt Whitman feels the need to make an inventory, to *catalogue* them. This he does: the very act of celebrating himself becomes an act of transformation, not of himself, but of the world of artifacts along the road where he passes, yawping his barbaric yawp. This counting of heads, this effort to assess the raw-material resources of the continent, becomes an act of poetry, an act of possessing all that he sees.

The pure contralto sings in the organ loft,
The carpenter dresses his plank, the tongue of his foreplane
  whistles its wild ascending lisp,
The married and unmarried children ride home to their Thanksgiving dinner. . . .

What appears to be no more than telling observation is an imaginative act of possession. The tongue of the fore plane spoke a language that the poet understood, and needed no elaboration, but the poet himself did not know how well he listened, and how clearly he saw. Good poetry and bad prose, with true democratic tolerance, share page after page. The raw material seems enough, just to catalogue it, to store it away in the mind for some future reference, some moment of tranquillity when the poet, at his ease, will fashion it into poetry. A moment, needless to say, that never comes.

The big thing was the beginning, the tremendous first

awareness, the first need to see it, feel it, and name it, the first hungry effort to grasp the horn of plenty and gorge on it. Whitman holds it above his head like a wineskin, squeezing it between his hands, letting the stream stain his mouth. That legendary hunger of our men in their youth, which reached its culmination in Wolfe, Whitman both experienced and put on record in "The Song of Myself." He dipped his hands into life, as into a sack of grain, and let the rich, golden stuff run lovingly between his fingers. He ran his long searching tongue, like that of an anteater, into the hidden cracks of life. And he found it—so he tells us with conviction—he found all of it good. Walt Whitman, turbulent, fleshy, sensual, eating, drinking and breeding, is the forerunner of those anonymous classics the Sears, Roebuck and Montgomery Ward catalogues. The poetry of things. The poetry of the sheer weight and number of things. The uses, abuses, and value of things, the appearance, description, and nature of things, the name and number of things, with their price, place, and listing in the great plan. This *mystique* of things was grasped and lucidly described by Henry James.

To be at all critically, or as we have been fond of calling it, analytically minded—over and beyond an inherent love of the many-colored picture of things—is to be subject to the superstition that objects and places, coherently grouped, disposed for human use and addressed to it, must have a sense of their own, a mystic meaning proper to themselves to give out: to give out, that is, to the participant at once so interested and so detached as to be moved to a report of the matter.

The mystic meaning proper to objects themselves is the poetry in Whitman. The mere sight of things, a listing of their uses, excites in the American a rudimentary aesthetic. It is not uniquely American, but as Americans we rely on it almost uniquely. After all, what *else* is there? Objects and places are the only things we have, and they bear such *mystique* meaning as we have to give out. The artifact, indeed, is as close as we get to folk poetry. In his *Let Us Now Praise Famous Men* James Agee makes this statement:

Meanwhile the floor, the roof, the opposed walls, the furniture, in their hot gloom: all watch upon one hollow center. The intricate tissue is motionless. The swan, the hidden needle, hold their course. On the red-gold wall sleeps a long, faded, ellipsoid smear of light. The base is dark. Upon the leisures of the earth the whole home is lifted before the approach of darkness as a boat and as a sacrament.

A century after the *Leaves of Grass,* and just fifty years later than James penned his observation, objects and places, coherently grouped, still give out their mystic meaning. The mind of Thoreau, and the mind of Whitman, the minds of Henry James, Fitzgerald, and Faulkner, are penetrated to the core by the light that radiates

from such artifacts. It is *this* prevailing tendency that
gives our literature a tone and texture that have charmed
the world, and nourished the illusion, necessary to the
world, that we are still the keepers of the promise. In
the *beginning*—our men of genius go on saying—this is
how it was. . . .

That raw-material world that Whitman loved so profoundly, and catalogued with such genius and affection,
gave way, in time, to a single, sensual, mystic piece of it—
the poet himself, radiant with meanings to give out. From
his poetry the world perceptibly recedes, objects and
places lose their contours, blend together, an abstraction
replaces the speech of the fore plane, with its wild ascending lisp. An almost tidal recession, a seaward drift of
artifacts, leaves the poet on the beach, like a bark that has
stranded, honed down by wind and sea to that essential
fact, Walt Whitman himself.

This is the man we see—and who so plainly sees us—
from so many photographs. The poet has become his own
poem. He never stops working on it. The homespun suit,
the shirt open at the throat, the old broadbrim hat with
the brim seduced, and at the center of the frame, beguil-
ing and beckoning, the affectionate gaze. Camerado, it
says, to one and to all, give me your hand.

The good gray poet, having become his own object,
having arranged and rearranged the lines of his figure,
looms before us in the lens, on the ground glass—but

dissolves as the shutter snaps. No matter how sweet the fat on a man's own bones—and there was none sweeter than Walt Whitman's—it is not the raw material through which the artist exceeds himself. Quite the contrary. When the poet is his own object, his own subject, the open road of the imagination is closed. Without the stars, the real stars, to chart its course by, the mind wanders in the labyrinth of self-awareness, its only raw material the sweet or bitter fat on its bones.

In his study of Walt Whitman, John Jay Chapman observes:

> If the roadside, the sky, the distant town, the soft buffeting of the winds of heaven, are a joy to the esthetic part of man, the freedom from all responsibility and accountability is Nirvana to his moral nature. . . . Life has no terrors for such a man. Society has no hold on him. The trifling inconveniences of the mode of life are as nothing compared to its satisfactions. The worm that never dies is dead in him. The great mystery of consciousness and of effort is quietly dissolved into the vacant happiness of sensation—not base sensation, but the sensation of the dawn and sunset, of the mart and the theatre, and the stars, and the panorama of the universe.

If we add that this universe appears to be new—new in the sense that it has been unobserved and unreported—we have the raw material that Walt Whitman, the Kosmos, discovered for himself. A Greek-like, dew-dappled morning freshness hovers over it. Old as some of it all too

plainly is, it strikes the poet as new. There it all lies!
Nobody has wooed it with song and words.

The blab of the pave, tires of carts, sluff of boot-soles, talk of
   the promenaders,
The heavy omnibus, the driver with his interrogating thumb, the
   clank of the shod horses on the granite floor,
The snow-sleighs, clinking, shouted jokes, pelts of snow-
   balls . . .

Each and everything must be mentioned. Each thing
in its place, with its own smell, look, and substance, each
thing curiously separate and yet at home among all
things, singing, we might say, as Blake's morning stars
would sing together. No blade of grass is too small, no
measureless orb is too big in this crowded heaven. In this
panoramic universe the poet is the axis.

It is not chaos or death—it is form, union, plan—it is eternal life
   —it is Happiness.

It is also self-intoxication, since form, union, and plan
are lacking. All that remains is the vacant happiness of
sensation, or Happiness, capitalized.

As technique and raw material blended together—
where, he would have asked, does one draw the line between them?—his powers as an artist, his sense of dis-
crimination, his ability to choose between one thing and
another—his intelligence—dissolved into sensation, and
sensation dissolved into the fat, none sweeter, that grew

on his own bones. To all those wonderful things once coherently grouped, once disposed for human use and addressed to it, to all those things he gave an affectionate, blurred farewell. In "The Song of Myself" he said:

There is that in me—I do not know what it is—but I know it is in me.

This marks the point where such poetry begins, but for Whitman that was where it ended, where it dissolves into sensations too vague and too grand to pin down. The latter-day Whitman, Thomas Wolfe, did not merely subscribe to such an observation, but wrote book after tremendous book attesting to it. There *was* something in him, but he never discovered what it was. On the evidence he left us, the great bone piles of his hunger, it was appetite. Art and technique begin where these idolators of the raw material seem to feel that it ends—with the sensations they have in the presence of the material. A poet of genius, Whitman's first impressions, the first dipping of his hands into the horn of plenty, lured him into song, but more a song of the world than of himself. As his self moved to the center of the picture, the center of his world, the song lost its music. He did not have the mind to see that for himself. He would have told you, if asked, What has *mind* to do with poetry? With the winds of heaven, the clouds, the sky, the dawn and the sunset, the body and the soul, and up there, beckoning,

the panorama of the universe. The mind, the mind he
would have told you, is a very small thing, just one of
many. But the mind of the poet is the one thing through
which the many exist. We do not know if Whitman read,
or what he would have made of, this passage from An-
drew Marvell:

Mean while the mind, from pleasure less,
Withdraws into its happiness:
The Mind, that Ocean where each kind
Does streight its own resemblance find;
Yet it creates, transcending these,
Far other Worlds, and other Seas;
Annihilating all that's made
To a green Thought in a green Shade.

It is such a mind, it is such an awareness, that marks
the poet who masters his subject, not the one who, mindless, permits himself to dissolve into it. In not being, as
a poet, analytically minded—over and beyond his love
of the many-colored picture of things—Whitman fell
subject to the superstition that the object of greatest interest was himself. It had a mystic meaning proper to itself
to give out. What the mystic meaning was, proper or
improper, neither the poet nor the reader will ever know,
since a report of the matter, both interested and detached,
was never made. Shortly before he died, however, in a
postscript to a letter, he sounded once again the same note:

More and more it comes to the fore that the only theory worthy of our modern times for g't literature, politics sociology must combine all the bulk-people of all lands, the women not forgetting. But the mustard plaster on my side is stinging & I must stop. Goodbye to all.

The bulk people of all lands, the women not forgetting, have in Whitman a voice almost equally blended of raw and processed material, the elements and the simply elemental, as life, in its general and shifting aspects, so often seems. This blend is the despair of the sophisticated critic, as it is of that fictive public, the bulk people, the latter disturbed by the poetry, the former by the corn. The poet's self-styled barbaric yawp has done much to conceal what is unique in his vision—the utterance of a man who stands entirely in the present, who is at home in shifting sands.

Here is the poet of the one-night stand. Each day is sufficient unto itself, each dawn ushers in a new world of experience, doctrines and dogmas are left by the wayside, the old skin is sheered off. D. H. Lawrence seemed to feel that this voice, and the open road down which it beckoned, challenged all men to enter the brave new world, and abandon the old. And so it did, in its fashion, but what do we see looming up ahead? Here is where the penetrating eyes of a native scans the road more knowingly than the tourist.

Walt Whitman [John Jay Chapman says] has given utterance to the soul of the tramp. A man of genius has passed sincerely and normally through this entire experience, himself unconscious of what he was, and he has left a record of it to enlighten and bewilder the world.

To enlighten and bewilder, almost in equal proportions, would seem to be the peculiar fate of the Good Gray Poet whose yawp continues to sound over the roofs of the world. But the poet who, singlehanded, returned the transcendental soul to its body, is *the* American poet whether Americans trouble to read him or not. His flight, his mythic open road, his comradely call to the great open spaces, is a poem that has become an industry. We are all tramps, in the modern manner, possessors of that new thing, active leisure, which promises to distract if not enlighten the bazaars of the world. That poet who tramped a perpetual journey still goes before us, scans the road maps with us, and whispers at the fork which is the almost-open road we should take. He is the prophet of the life that is as modern as tomorrow, the open road of flight.

FIVE

THE HIGH SEAS

HERMAN MELVILLE

O brothers, who through a hundred thousand perils have reached the west, to this so brief vigil of the senses that remains to us choose not to deny experience, in the sun's track, of the unpeopled world. Take thought of the seed from which you spring. You were not born to live as brutes, but to follow virtue and knowledge.

This outcry of Dante, in the name of Ulysses—in the name of the pagan he must condemn—is perhaps the classic statement of the call of the sea. To this brief vigil of the senses that remains, do not deny adventure, experience, and knowledge. Take thought of your manhood. Live as a man and not as a brute.

That the figure of Ulysses should arouse, in such diverse natures as Tennyson and Dante, the most intense flights of their poetry indicates the depths to which this archetypal adventurer appeals in Western man. On the one hand, God, a world of coherent virtues and vices, on the other the challenge of the unknowable. The schism is classic. The mind seems so divided within itself. In our own time it is the gap that lies between such natures as T. S. Eliot and D. H. Lawrence: no persuasion will reconcile these opposing worlds. In Dante, at this juncture, they meet, and although the mind of Dante is a mighty fortress, erected to bear witness to the power of God, it is here that we sense this mind is divided within itself. He must condemn the pagan's motives, and his sinful pride—but the poet's heart goes with him, nevertheless. For who else, who but Dante, had so profoundly hungered after virtue and knowledge and understood so well the brief vigil of the senses here on earth? This outcry is a passionate expression of the free part of his soul: the Godlike mere man, the pagan adventurer, blessed with nothing but his pride, his hunger, and his talents, out to follow the sun's track to wherever it might lead.

Dante is obliged to bring this pagan to heel, but, like the souls of those doomed lovers, Paolo and Francesca, his ruin seems to make him more deeply a part of us. However unwilling, or unaware, the poet is here more profound than the theologian, and it is in the lower regions of his world that we find the souls we love.

But without the sea—the mirror of the sea—the appeal of Ulysses would lose some of its force. The deserts, the mountains, and even the plains call men, but it seems to be the sea, real or imaginary, that speaks to them in such a metaphysical voice. Man is seldom led to think that he goes there in search of the facts, or even how to live. No, he goes there in search of some notion of himself.

That is the positive side of an impulse that has its less admirable appeal—one also goes to sea just to get away, to get away from it *all*. Even one's own kind become abstractions, familiar routine functions rather than personalities, since the mirror of the sea reflects nothing but the viewer and itself. And if one wants to be alone, try sailing alone. Try sailing alone around the world. It is no accident that an American, Captain Joshua Slocum, was the first man to have done what even wily Ulysses would not have thought of doing. Slocum was born in 1844, just a year before Thoreau pitched his camp at Walden, and Herman Melville, an ordinary seaman, was homeward bound from Honolulu on the *United States*. Americans were beginning to get around, that is; to get away from it all.

From Slocum to Lindbergh—from the end of sail to the beginning of flight, a revolution in the space of twenty-five years—the word that enthralled the imagination was the word "alone." Sailing alone around the world, and flying alone to Paris. These acts of defiance, both unaware and deliberate, reveal the individual's sense of predicament in a world that is now overpopulated with both people and things. *Flight* always cuts two ways; it is both toward something and away from something—but perhaps the sea, the symbol of unknowing, is the ideal field of action for both impulses. In getting away from it all, from all that is not self, that is not real-seeming, that is not real living, man is obliged to confront the lonely facts of self-awareness, the true-false image of himself the mirror of the sea affords. Flight and the impossibility of flight meet in the high loft of the crow's nest. There are few facts to record, few incidents to beguile the mind from its *self*. All around, in an eternal flux, the light plays on the mirror of the sea, inviting and demanding that a man loaf at his ease, and consort with his soul.

> Surely [Melville observes], all this is not without meaning. And still deeper the meaning of that story of Narcissus, who because he could not grasp the tormenting, wild image he saw in the fountain, plunged into it and was drowned. But that same image, we ourselves see in all rivers and oceans. It is the image of the ungraspable phantom of life: and this is the key to it all.

If not the key to it all, it would seem to be the key to most of Melville. It was the way he had, in the words of Ishmael, of driving off the spleen and regulating the circulation, of getting rid of, or nursing, the drizzly November in his soul.

Between 1851 and 1856, *Moby Dick, Walden,* and *Leaves of Grass* were published—three books that had in common their sense of isolation and the need, of the authors, to regulate the circulation. Books and authors seem to have appeared, and to have run their course, without benefit of each other. If we recall that this culture—that of New York and New England—was then something of a tight little island, the isolation of these men, and their works, is all the more remarkable. We know that Emerson spoke out boldly for Whitman, and that Whitman was a reader of Thoreau, but these are exceptions that point up the rule. Isolation, indeed, is the spirit of the place, and it is what we find in both the books and the authors. It is already, that is, a lonely crowd. Each man is engaged in a lonely crusade. They take to the woods, to the open road, or to the high seas, as single men. Walt Whitman appears to give the lie to this observation with his call to comrades, but first, last, and always, when his song is convincing, it is of himself he sings. Isolation was the spirit of the place, and it was against such a spirit that Whitman, with his slogans and his genius, lived out his rebellion.

I celebrate myself, says one; Call me Ishmael, says another; and the third speaks at length as to what it was that took him, alone, to the woods.

Besides the isolation, the spirit of the place, a man born of woman would notice something else. These lonely men were not in pursuit of women: it was not the *Ewig-Weibliche,* even in the form of a pond or a whale, that lured them on. Walt Whitman, gross, mystical nude, the man who returned the body to the transcendental soul, included woman in his vast inventory, but she was no more, and no less, than a thousand other objects within his new world.

. . . not a person or object missing,
Absorbing all to myself and for this song.

Thoreau's passion for facts, Whitman's passion for objects saturated with life, and Melville's passion for truth, are various aspects of the raw-material chaos that confronted them. Life was abundant but incoherent: the facts had not been ordered, the things had not been named. To know the facts, one went to the woods; to name the things, one took to the road; and to brood on the meaning of it all, one took to sea. Common to all these pursuits was the raw-material wilderness that called for taming, and the fact that whatever one sought, one sought for it somewhere *else*. You had to leave the city, the society, and the comforts of home to look for it.

Born the same year as Whitman, and a true son of Manhattan, as Whitman was not, Melville early showed the prevailing tendency of his countrymen. But it was the sea, not the wilderness, to which he was drawn. The hard facts of his life were metaphysical, the phantom of life he sought to grasp was ungraspable, and a profound intuition turned him from the landed wilderness to the uncharted seas. It provided the stage for precisely such players as he cared to put on it, and a permanently congenial setting for the drizzly November that never left his soul. The man who had "pretty much made up his mind to be annihilated," had found his subject, and as much of his *self* as he cared to fish from the briny deeps.

But metaphysical *facts* are hard to come by. It may be this knowledge, this foreknowledge, that sends the seeker to sea for them. The isolation at sea, the prophetic blending of security and flight, order and freedom, fact and fancy, symbolized the tension, and the metaphysical woods, at the core of Melville's mind. His thinking began at the beginning, and he attempted to resolve the unresolved problems, to hew the raw truth out of a world of discordant facts. This metaphysical agony, generated by the sea and such a fermenting mind as Shakespeare's, also nourished and sustained his impulse to be annihilated. That seemed to be one *fact* of life. In a conversation with Hawthorne he confided his soul's predicament:

He had [Hawthorne reported], pretty much made up his mind to be annihilated, but still he does not rest in that anticipation: and I think he will never rest until he gets hold of a definite belief. It is strange how he persists—and has persisted ever since I knew him, and probably long before—in wandering to and fro over these deserts, as dismal and monotonous as the sand hills amid which we were sitting. He can neither believe, nor be comfortable in his unbelief: and he is too honest and courageous not to try to do one or the other. If he were a religious man, he would be one of the most truly religious and reverential: he has a very high and noble nature, and better worth immortality than most of us.

If Hawthorne had substituted the monotonous waves of the sea for those of the sands hills in which they were sitting, the melancholy wanderer would have been anchored in his natural setting. The monotonous nature of his obsession—the metaphysical wastes of belief and disbelief—would have come to nothing without his native instinct for the artifact. The concrete object, afloat in his metaphysics, was a whale. The pursuit of this whale was narration, and the play of whaling facts and metaphysics, shot through with real spray and strands of action, made of *Moby Dick* the mirror in which he reflected the most of his *self*. "I have written a wicked book," he wrote to Hawthorne, "and feel white as a lamb."

But the feeling soon passed. It did not do for him what it has the power to do for some of its readers— serve as a key, however inscrutable, to the mystery of life.

I had some vague idea [he wrote to Mrs. Hawthorne], while writing it, that the whole book was susceptible of some allegorical construction, and also that parts of it were—but the specialty of many of the particular subordinate allegories, were first revealed to me after reading Hawthorne's letter, which, without citing any particular examples, yet intimated the part-and-parcel allegoricalness of the whole.

As Leon Howard, in his biography of Melville, has pointed out, Melville was neither the first nor the last writer between Isaiah and Thomas Mann to have such an experience. "It is, in fact," Mr. Howard goes on to say, "a normal one for an author who uses the kind of symbolism found in Moby Dick. For a symbol is an imaginative bridge between the general and the particular which may be crossed in either direction; and Melville, having tried without much satisfaction in *Mardi* the method of expressing a general conception in a specific image, had gradually slipped into the practice of letting his mind play around *concrete details* until they were made luminous with suggestive implications." [Italics mine]

Certain facts of good and evil, that is, the essential raw facts of metaphysical experience, were processed in the same way in which Thoreau, standing face to face with the facts of Walden, saw the sun glimmer on their surfaces, and felt the sweet edge dividing him through the heart and the marrow. Both men craved this essential, however illusive, reality. Both made the search for such facts their lonely business, reported only such truths as they happened to find, and much of the ground that we stand on, metaphysical and concrete, was the work of their imaginations.

As he gathered the countless *facts* in his *Journal,* as he patiently waited for the *essential* fact to suddenly illuminate the others, Thoreau set the pattern for all future gatherers of data—a belief in what one might *find*, rather than in what one must conjure up.

In his catalogue of objects, lovingly apprehended and poetically labeled, Whitman exercised the same commitment to *things*—the hallmark of his genius—but the transformation of things, the function of such genius, he left to the caprice of the occasion. Things might or might not—and they increasingly did not—generate in him the maximum intensity, largely because he seemed unaware that such intensity was desired. Nostalgia took the place of imaginative possession: reminiscence took the place of apprehension. In both Whitman and Thoreau, the gathering of *data*, the granaries of the mind stuffed with facts and objects, became a substitute for that immaterial thing the imaginative act. In such garrulity, whether in public poems or private journals, there is less density than in silence, and that is where we find it. In the silence of Melville, rather than in his expression, we find the crisis of the American imagination. Raw material and *im*-material, technique and imagination, reach an impasse in the expressive silence of Melville. When this silence is finally broken it is instructive. The last window of Melville's fiction opens on the past, and it is not, he warns us, fiction pure and simple. His final word, in *Billy Budd*, is in the form of a historical incident—not a story, he took the pains to remind us, because "The sym-

metry of form attainable in pure fiction cannot so readily
be achieved in a narration essentially having less to do
with fable than with fact."

This observation, no matter how we construe it, sums
up the state of the American imagination after a century
of engagements, most of them inconclusive, with the raw
material of American experience. If what you want is the
truth, with its ragged edges, stick to the facts. And the
facts? You will find them recorded in the past. As Melville did, for his tale of Billy Budd, as Thoreau did, in
the artifacts of Walden, as Whitman did nearly everywhere he looked, and as Mark Twain thought he did,
certainly, in that song of himself, *Huckleberry Finn.* Not
the American past, or just the past in general, but the
one that existed beyond the long arm of suspicion—one's
own personal past, the beginning of everything. When
Twain staked out his own boyhood, the raw-material
inventory was complete. The real world lay *behind* him,
as it lies behind all of us. Back there, safe from the long
arm of Aunt Sally, lay the territory ahead.

THE AVAILABLE PAST

MARK TWAIN

And yet I can't go away from the boyhood period and write because capital (that is, personal experience) is not sufficient by itself and I lack the other essential: interest in handling the men and experience of later times.   —Deleted from a letter to
an unidentified person.

The man who marks the spot where our literature began, according to Ernest Hemingway, is the author of two world classics about boys. *Tom Sawyer* is about boys, for boys; *Huckleberry Finn* is about boys, for men. Mark Twain ran the gamut of life from Tom Sawyer to Huckleberry Finn. This, as he put it himself, was his capital. In America it was not a small thing. From a boyhood idyl of the good life to a boy's criticism of that life is the natural range and habitat of the American mind. The green breast of the world at its greenest to the breast of that world at its brownest is roughly the line of descent from Twain to Hemingway. The Mississippi and the Big Two-Hearted River represent the starting points,

soon defiled, the past that is exploited and corrupted, and
Hemingway's exile is a judgment on things as they are;
the green dream burned over, the clear streams polluted,
the natural beauty corrupted beyond repair. From a myth
of inexhaustible resources we move to a myth of all resources exhausted. It is all or nothing, and nothing is the
myth of the hard-boiled age.

We need not challenge the accuracy of Hemingway's
judgment to understand its source. In both Hemingway
and Twain it lies in their boyhood: a timeless river idyl
for that young rebel Huckleberry Finn; for Hemingway the Big Two-Hearted River deep in the Michigan
woods. An affinity more intimate than style, a brotherhood of great promise and quick disillusion, unites the
young men of *The Sun Also Rises* with the skeptical idyl
of Huckleberry Finn. In both, we must remember, there
is no green territory up *ahead*. Up there lies Aunt Sally,
with her civilizing ways, and we know about that. Small
wonder that Hemingway, fifty years later, should leap
into exile like a trout—the old world rather than the new
representing the territory ahead. It is what, we can rest
assured, Huck Finn would have done. The past itself
has receded, the green world no longer lay in the wild
blue yonder but in the minds of the men, of the artists
who had dreamed it up. It was in Art, the world of
master craftsmen, that Hemingway found the green light
that lured him on, with war the raw material most

congenial to his mind. The destruction of the things in which one believes—the corruption and abuse of America's green promise—has been the subject of his work since *In Our Time*. In the battle of the old man and the sea, in his triumph and defeat, Hemingway confronted and resolved the dilemma that Mark Twain was unable to face. He gave a man's answer to Twain's question, *What is Man?* Faced with this problem, the two worlds of Huck Finn and Tom Sawyer were of little help, and in reply to the question *What is Man?*, Twain tells us what a boy is. One born in Florida, Missouri, who knew life on the Mississippi, roughed it in the West, was an innocent abroad, and returned to win and lose a fortune and wonder what is man. In *The Mysterious Stranger*, Tom Sawyer, grown old, makes his peace.

It is true, that which I have revealed to you; there is no God, no universe, no human race, no earthly life, no heaven, no hell. It is all a dream—a grotesque and foolish dream. Nothing exists but you. And you are nothing but a *thought*—a vagrant thought, a useless thought, a homeless thought, wandering forlorn among the empty eternities!

This vision of life might have come to Huck Finn —we are obliged to say that it did—after his wandering to and fro in the world, in search of the mythic territory. The words that Twain chooses to characterize the unspeakable mystery are revealing: a vagrant, useless, and homeless thought, a boy, that is, cut off from his ties, from his dreams, from even the reassuring horror of Aunt Sally, left to wander like a child among the empty eternities.

Huck Finn's pilgrimage—the boy who lit out for the territory ahead, but never found it—is the true-to-life story of Mark Twain. A natural—a man who learned to write the way a river pilot learns the feel of a channel —he had the *capital*, he was well equipped, he thought, for the writer's trade.

Saturated with facts of a raw-material nature, but isolated from facts of a cultural nature, the cultural isolation proved to be the most irreparable. The *facts* of life— loss of money, loss of youth, loss of loved ones—left Twain, as it does all men, with less and less facts, and more and more thoughts. But a *thought*—a thought was the one fact he could not trust. This cultural fact, more durable since more immaterial, seemed to contradict the world of raw-material facts in which he was at home. His innocence, of which he made capital in his many ventures abroad, ended by making him an exile from both worlds, the mythic facts of his boyhood and the cultural facts of his manhood, leaving him to wander forlorn in a world without a God, without a Universe, without Aunt Sally.

It may seem hard to believe that Henry James and Mark Twain were *contemporaries*. If the word both seems and is something of a paradox in connection with them, it is a frequent paradox in the American scene. Men alive at the same time do not necessarily live in the same age. Between the natural phenomenon, like Twain, and the cultural phenomenon, like James, there may lie a stretch of time similar to the stretch of the continent. The essential paradox of these two men of genius, of Life on the Mississippi with the Life in the Mind of James, is that between raw material and technique, between nonconsciousness and supreme consciousness carried to one of its peaks. What is singular, perhaps unique, is that this should occur on American soil, that only American experience will begin to account for it. The exile of James was a deliberate and highly conscious effort of possession, *re*possession, that is, of what James considered his inheritance. He sought to be, and became, a supremely conscious American. Nothing could better illustrate the raw-material range and promise of the American imagination than the thought of Henry James meeting Mark Twain, an innocent abroad. The innocent doing his level best to dispense with all that highfalutin cultural nonsense, at the moment that James was trying to bring the new world to terms with it.

In this imaginary encounter of James and Twain, the cultural fact and the natural fact, the supreme technician and the natural yarn spinner, we have the two poles, the opposing worlds of American sensibility. The man who had the equipment, all of it real, since he had none of it from books, and the man who knew that books contained the indispensable capital. What Mark Twain needed the most was what he went abroad to ridicule. The old world had been processed so many times that the raw-material savor had gone out of it, but Twain did not know that the *process* was the thing, that the process, not nature, put the savor back into it. But the traveler from Missouri saw nothing in the cultural facts but the ruins.

In James, the supremely self-conscious artist, and Twain, the supremely unconscious natural talent, the limits of technique and raw material come face to face. Knowing what he was doing, knowing with a knowledge he could share with no one but his "blest old Genius," James persisted, to his last breath, in doing what he must. Not knowing what he was doing, never truly having known, Twain soon gave it up. He distracted himself with a series of books for growing boys. He began, he was always beginning, a fresh start, a boy's clear-eyed look at the world around his boyhood—a look that had no outlook, a boy who was obliged to never grow up. In the dreamy, shifting mirror of the Mississippi, fiction and fact softly blurred at the edges. But in one moment of vision, a state of hallowed reminiscence, he seemed to grasp the distinction, his genius flowed into it. Into *Life on the Mississippi* he poured the facts; into *Huckleberry Finn* he poured the fiction. Having done so, he lost all

awareness of what he had done. In each case, as it appears
to us now, the memory was processed by the same emotion—a dream of nostalgia centered on a growing boy,
and on a growing young man. But the eternal river, the
majestic river seen through the eyes of both of these
travelers, from a steamboat or a raft, turns out to be
pretty much the same. *Both* rivers are fiction. They have
been processed, that is, into permanence. At this moment,
at this critical juncture of raw material and the imagination, Mark Twain, the great natural, joined hands with
that genius of artifice, Henry James.

Since the literature of the world affords us no finer
example of raw material in the process of becoming fiction, it will pay to observe how this is done. In the nineteenth chapter of *Huckleberry Finn,* the boy out on the
raft describes what he sees in this manner:

The first thing to see, looking away over the water, was a
kind of dull line—that was the woods on t'other side: you
couldn't make anything else out; then a pale place in the sky,
then more paleness spreading around, then the river softened up
away off, and warn't black anymore, but gray; you could see
the little dark spots drifting along ever so far away—trading
scows, and such things; and long black streaks, rafts; sometimes
you could hear a sweep creaking; or jumbled up voices, it was so
still, and sounds came so far; and bye and bye you could see a
streak on the water which you know by the look of the streak
that there's a snag there in the swift current which breaks on it

and makes that streak look that way; and you see the mist curl up off the water, and the east reddens, and the river, and you make out a log cabin on the edge of the woods, away on the bank on t'other side of the river, being a woodyard likely, and piled by them cheats so you can throw a dog through it any-wheres; then the nice breeze springs up, and comes fanning you from over there, so cool and fresh and sweet to smell on account of the woods and the flowers; but sometimes not that way, be-cause they've left dead fish laying around, gars and such, and they do get pretty rank; and next you've got the full day, and everything smiling in the sun, and the song-birds just going it!

As fine as this is, it is the memory of a man, processed to appear as the vision of a boy. A citizen of Hartford, a husband and good provider, who chooses to remember what he fancies he misses, the smell of woods and flowers, and the songbirds just going it. There is knowledge acquired later, as a river pilot, put into the language of a boy, and a man's emotion is processed to suit the substance of his memory.

If now we turn to *Life on the Mississippi*, to the *facts*, that is, we find this:

Now when I had mastered the language of this water and had come to know every trifling feature that bordered the great river as familiarly as I knew the letters of the alphabet, I had made a valuable acquisition. But I had lost something too. I had lost something which could never be restored to me while I lived. All the grace, the beauty, the poetry, had gone out of the majestic river! I still kept in mind a certain wonderful sunset which I witnessed when steamboating was new to me. A broad expanse of the river was turned to blood; in the middle distance the red hue brightened into gold, through which a solitary log came floating, black and conspicuous; in one place a long slanting mark lay sparkling upon the water; in another the surface was broken by boiling, tumbling rings, that were as many tinted as an opal; where the ruddy flush was faintest, was a smooth spot that was covered with graceful circles and radiating lines, ever so delicately traced; the shore on our left was densely wooded and the somber shadow that fell from this forest was broken in one place by a long, ruffled trail that shone like silver; and high above the forest wall a clean-stemmed dead tree waved a single leafy bough that glowed like a flame in the unobstructed splendor that was flowing from the sun. There were graceful curves, reflected images, woody heights, soft distances, and over the whole scene, far and near, the dissolving lights drifted steadily, enriching it every passing moment with new marvels of coloring.

We are on the same river. We are close, indeed, to being on the same raft. Once the wealth of the impressions starts to flow, once this lyrical fountainhead is tapped, the prose flows like the river, without interruption, merely snagged here and there by commas and semicolons, but too grand and majestically alive to be stopped by something like a period. Man and boy, on steamboat or raft, the writer is in a state of intoxication, but he remains on his feet, his senses clairvoyant, with a firm hand on the flow of his impressions. His spirit trembles at such beauty, but he gives us a controlled, lucid report. For man and boy the river is the thing, the source from which the fact and the fiction flows, but for the man, alas, it is a passing thing. He first tells us as much. In his mastery of the river he had lost more than he had gained. He had lost, he tells us, what could never again be restored to him. Was this *why*, we might ask, was this *how*, from amidst the wilderness of his nostalgia, he was able to conjure up this river of permanence? One that he would not, like that dreamy cub pilot, grow up and grow old and lose forever; or find that the grace, the beauty and the poetry had all gone out of it! What we do know is that it is here, in the grip of this passion for what has escaped him, that the emotion has processed the memory into art. What that boy, Huck Finn, had lost through knowledge, through the territory of life ruled over by Aunt Sally, the man was able to recover in this lucid moment of reminiscence and craft. It was the knowledge of the loss—the man's knowledge—that generated what was timeless in the boy's impressions. No more beautiful or instructive example of the artist's dilemma, of the source of his passions, and how, if ever, he must lovingly resolve them, is available to us than this passion of Mark Twain, resolved in *Huckleberry Finn*.

Brooding on the river, brooding on the very experience that deprived him of his early dew-dappled enchantment, Twain was able to regain the Paradise that he had given up for lost. But there is reason to believe that he remained unaware of this. His *Life on the Mississippi*, the mature reflections that inspired what was best in his writing, represented to him, as it did to most of his readers, a much more important book than *Huckleberry Finn*. This was truly a man's book, not just a boy's, and no less a figure than John Hay wrote him to say as much.

It is perfect—no more nor less. I don't see how you do it. I knew all that, every word of it—passed as much time on the levee as you ever did, knew the same crowd, saw the same scenes —but I could not have remembered one word of it all. You have the two greatest gifts of a writer, memory and imagination.

The order of the words is important. Memory *and* imagination. What John Hay, as well as Mark Twain, like all the sensible men of their time appreciated, was first of all the *facts*—and Twain seemed to have the facts right. If he wanted to embroider them a little with his humor, with his talent for dialect and description, that was fine. And they would marvel how he did it. And they did. *Huckleberry Finn* was a book for boys; *Life on the Mississippi* was a book for men, especially men who had been there and could judge for themselves.

In this prevailing judgment Mark Twain would concur. Although his imagination had restored to him what he had given up for lost—afforded him possession of it for the first time—his sensible down-to-earth mind remained convinced that it was the facts, the lost facts, that truly mattered. The great majestic river, like his boyhood, was lost to him forever. Knowledge and experience —those disillusioning specters—had muddied the waters of the river of life. The deplorable world of Aunt Sally— the ordeal of Mark Twain with Hartford and Mrs. Clemens—left nothing but staleness and disenchantment in its wake. At the moment, his creative mind hung in the balance, imagining the green morning of the world in *Huckleberry Finn*, his conscious practical mind, brooding on the sorry facts, had already relegated the past to limbo. The good old days, and the great majestic river, were gone. Nothing remained to him but debts, business ventures, and failures, trips abroad and flights of fancy, the loss of his loved ones, and the raw-material bankruptcy of *What is Man?* And what was he?

Stripped of his imagination, Henry James could have told him, he was not much.

Part Three

THE BRIDGE

SEVEN

USE OF THE PAST

HENRY JAMES

I know what I am about, and I have always my eyes on my
native land.   —Letter to William James

In Henry James, America had come of age fifty years
before Van Wyck Brooks, surveying the field, wrote his
challenging essay suggesting that this had taken place.
A rallying point for all home-grown talents, for whom
it seemed to clear the air and set the clock forward, it
set the clock backward in failing to come to terms with
James. The one American genius who *had* come of age,
who had, that is, more than parochial standards, Brooks
consigned to the limbo of native talents who had fallen
under foreign domination, a rootless man, whose work
naturally suffered from its rootlessness.

The habit of exile, which many modern artists have
found congenial, for various reasons, Brooks interpreted
as a simple lack of faith in America. But a decade before
Joyce, Proust, and that race of craftsmen who found in

93

art the coherence that the age had destroyed, James had established the example of the artist's life in his art. Since he did this without the usual Bohemian trappings, and lived the life of a gentleman of leisure, it went unobserved. Here again his genius, his virtues, and his defects isolated him from his contemporaries, although a small coterie paid court to his presence, his formidable personality. As Ford Madox Ford aptly remarked:

In the meantime, magisterially and at leisure, in Rye, Henry James was performing the miracles after whose secrets we were merely groping.

Neither Joyce nor Proust, with their hermetic passions, was more profoundly alone than Henry James, the exile who never took his eyes off his native land. Alone with his "poor blest old Genius," alone, and, as he knew, dying, he wrote to Henry Adams:

It's, I suppose, because I am that queer monster, the artist, an obstinate finality, an inexhaustible sensibility. . . . It all takes doing—and I *do*. I believe I shall do yet again—it is still an act of life.

He was always explaining; there was always the need for explanation, first for what he was up to, then for what he had done, so that even his dear old friends were convinced that he explained too much. Wasn't it clear he was not at all sure of himself? Now that the craft of fiction stands, insofar as it stands, in the clearing he made in the wilderness, we can see that his anxiety sprang from his love, from a passion at once so interested and so detached that he was moved to a report of the matter, a final touch, if one were needed, to his unceasing work in progress, the portrait of the artist as an inexhaustible sensibility.

The charge that James lacked raw material—raw in the sense that we recognize it in *Huckleberry Finn,* *Wuthering Heights,* and *Anna Karenina*—is often abused in its application, but probes near the heart of his defect as a "novelist." The material seems missing: it is the *im*material we find in his books. If that, indeed, is his purpose, and the very nature of his genius, there is a point, nevertheless, in the novel, where such powers of transformation strain the very illusion they seek to create. It is why the "question" of Henry James will persist. His experience was wide and intense, but it lacked the focus of a hopeless commitment. His passion was his craft, but out of craft one cannot conjure up *the* grand passion. It is here that life exercises its precedence over art.

In James we have the artist who apprehended much of life without the crippling effects of having lived it. His is the voice that says, "I know, I know," as we start to tell him of a personal disaster—and he does *know,* but often without the crushing aftereffects of such knowledge. He remains free to generalize; too free for the novelist.

In every writer of genius some limiting factor proves

to be essential to the growth of his gifts: in James it is an awareness so acute that it made experience unnecessary. What he called the "vibration" was not merely not enough, but more than that was too much. The seismograph of his genius recorded every tremor, but was not intended to register the local earthquakes. The "virus of suggestion," with its accompanying fever, was enough. In possessing a sensibility so rare that raw material, crude experience, seemed hardly necessary, James had to conjure up a novel where the immaterial would take its place. This he succeeded in doing, at no time failing to "consider life directly and closely," the immaterial becoming, in his hands, the material with the maximum density. He knew by divination, and what he knew was more important than the clumsy mechanics of experience itself. But such powers, however distinguished, may fatally handicap the man who writes novels, unless he creates the forms, and the standards, by which he must be judged. This is what James did in his late novels, and in the Prefaces. What might have proved a fatal defect he made the substance of his art.

His subject, no matter what the object, was consciousness. We may reasonably wonder, on the evidence, if human sensibility ever reached such a pitch of awareness as in the mind of James. It is here we find the root of his style—parenthesis. The mind of James, opening like a flower at the virus of suggestion, gives off and receives a series of vibrations that find their resolution in parenthesis. Nothing is closed. Closure means a loss of consciousness. One thing always leads to another, that in turn to another, and this play of nuances, like ripples lapping on a pond, is the dramatis personae of James, the novelist. His subject was his own ceaselessly expanding consciousness.

In the late books this is darkest James, but what appears impenetrable, even on examination, is the appalling density of one luminous mind. Here, before our eyes, consciousness is literally made visible. To *like* it calls for something more than a taste for it. Before Joyce, before Proust, the old man who was bent on explaining too much had immersed himself in the destructive element. Speaking of the *Golden Bowl*, Stephen Spender observed:

. . . one begins to feel certain that beneath the stylistic surface . . . there lurk forms of violence and chaos. His technical mastery has the perfection of frightful balance and frightful tension: beneath the stretched-out compositions there are abysses of despair and disbelief: *Ulysses* and *The Waste Land*.

The central defect in the mind and art of James is a defect of riches—he is simply too much for us. In James, and in James alone, the prevailing tendency of Thoreau's countrymen did not prevail. He did not take to the woods, to the open road, to his idyllic childhood, or to the high seas. He went east and not west. He took to the wilderness of culture, instead. The young and talented aesthete, who at twenty-two reviewed and dispensed with Whitman's barbaric yawp, had a lot to learn about both the old world and the new. He was buoyant on the high and rolling seas of the fashionable cliché. Fashion took him abroad—fashion made it natural for him to go—but it was not fashion that led him to stay. He was the first, of course, to both sense and define his predicament. With his customary insistence on the nuance, since that alone would give him the correct shade of meaning, he coined a word to describe his situation.

The word "*dis*patriot" carries the same charge, and much the same meaning, as the word "disinterested." It was *dis*interest that encouraged real interest. It was *dis*-patriation that encouraged patriation. Expatriate he became when sentiment and passion led him to throw in *his* lot with England—his America, that is—when she felt she was threatened with barbarism. It is likely that his sensitivity to the charge that he had left America led him to coin certain remarks to the contrary—but the place to look for his dispatriation is not in his rejoinders, but in his works. There it is clear that his exile was less a problem for him than it is for us. The question of his exile, if it still exists, is rooted in the need some Americans feel to rid themselves of a problem they do not like, a problem too deep and too thorny to be ignored or absorbed.

James is the archetype of this problem, brought up from our own depths to goad and haunt us, a now-immortal reminder of our fear and distrust of real intelligence. In leaving the country he almost spared us the trouble of *exiling* him. But he was intelligent; even more, he was a writer and craftsman of genius, incurably engaged in the art and practice of prophecy. So he came back—never truly having been away. The only writer who had not taken to the woods, he alone confronted the new culture of cities. He confronted and described the new *business* culture, with its downtown men and its uptown women, its out-of-town children, and its mindless cultural problems. The busy, the tipsy, and Daniel Webster still ruled —but there were changes. What were they? Were they for the better, or the worse?

Of Lady Barberina he wrote:

It was not in the least of American barbarism that she was afraid. Her dread was all of American civilization.

This will stand as one indictment he never departed from. It was not our barbarism, but our civilization that gave him dread.

In his insistence on the *facts*, on the real *virus*, on the need to observe it closely and directly, James shared a common instinct with Twain, Whitman, and Thoreau. In a letter to the Deerfield Summer School he said:

Tell the ladies and gentlemen, the ingenious inquirers, to consider life directly and closely, and not to be put off with mean and puerile falsities, and be conscientious about it.

But in beginning with the facts, he did not mean to
end with them. In James the beginning is only the beginning—the virus of suggestion induced the fever, and the
fever induced a state of heightened consciousness. From
that point on it was all imagination and technique. For
those who wanted the sock, his pulling on the yarn until
the sock had unraveled was something like a deliberate
abuse of the facts. It is the sock they want, the real sock,
and not the ball of yarn. In the genius of James—one of
the few on whom nothing, no, nothing, was lost—the
factual sock is a symbol of life going about its clumsy,
stupid business. The purpose of the artist is to unravel
the meaning of it. In James, as in Joyce, technique so
dominates the material as to lead one to wonder if the
material itself is still there. It is if one thinks of the run:
it is not if one thinks of the sock.

The technique of James, the modern aspect of it, is
the almost interminable unraveling. In this he anticipates
the compulsive mania of Proust and Joyce. The fashionable resemblance that the books of James bore to the
novels of the period, the *haut monde* strain of fiction,
eased the blow at the start, but eventually worked against
him. The suspicion inevitably emerged that his books
were *not* among them. If not, what, then, was he up to?
Nobody really knew. His readers diminished; his coterie
of old friends was tolerant. But at this point his enemies
moved into the open, and H. G. Wells, speaking with

their voice but with his own malice, lambasted the Master, whose sorry example might mislead the young.

For not writing books like other people—books madly disquieting in their uniqueness—James lived long enough to pay the penalty. He paid it doubly through his exile, since the lowest blows came from England, rather than from that quarter from which he most expected them. Full knowledge of his situation—having no country but the one he had created—led him to write the Prefaces, a unique *apologia pro vita sua,* before the need for such "artistic" apologies became fashionable.

A more civilized man is inconceivable, but the Prefaces speak for all men whose devotion to art made them Bohemians, cranks, or exiles. The nature of his own exile he may not have grasped—that of a man of genius in a world of business—since the note of persuasion, rather than rebellion, distinguishes all he had to say on this subject. The "manifesto" state of mind, in formation at the time, would have struck him as barbarous. He achieved his revolution with his hat on his head, wearing his gloves. This "figure" of James—the gentleman of fashion out of fashion—cut him off, even more than his genius, from the left bank Bohemianism of the new "art" —little of it as new, and even less of it as distinguished, as what he had been producing, alone, at Rye. The younger men who should have known did not know; he was in no van, he promoted no cult, and had come under the fire of the big solid guns that protect all men from a fate worse than death—a new experience.

This paragon, however, had the defects of his formidable gifts. Raw material, an excess of which handicapped or silenced his American contemporaries, had been processed into an immaterial essence, an orchestration of vibrations that dodged no issue, but reduced all issues to parentheses. In his decorous handling or nonhandling of sex, the raw-material litmus test, we sometimes have technique as a substitute for the material itself. It is immaterial, in the terms of this inquiry, whether more *experience* would have increased his power as a novelist. I think not. It would merely have increased *that* parenthesis. It was the nature of his gift to apprehend experience in the terms of vibrations, and sex—what he referred to as "the great relation between men and women, the constant world renewal"—would have been processed in the same manner as everything else. The mind of James, in this particular and many others, seems to parallel the process we see in physics, where the pursuit of reality ends in a magnetic field of waves. Nor do I feel this correspondence is misleading, however contrasting the demonstrations, since both processes are concerned with the expansion of consciousness. A universe in the making and the theories of Planck and Einstein found their correspondence in all of the arts, the most impressively, perhaps, in the new world of painting, where the object was dissolved, or broken up and put together according to a new plan. Joyce's experiments with language, Proust's with time, Whitehead's with process and reality, are all aspects of the evolution of the new consciousness. In the field of human sensibility there is James. The massif central of his awareness, the play of light and shadow in his consciousness offer a paradigm, in the field of literature, of the stupefying complex of the human mind, one aspect of which Sir Charles Sherrington describes in these words:

Should we continue to watch the scheme we should observe after a time an impressive change which suddenly accrues. In the great head-end which has been mostly darkness spring up myriads of twinkling stationary lights and myriads of trains of moving lights of many different directions. It is as though activity from one of those local places which continued restless in the darkened main-mass suddenly spread far and wide and invaded all. The great topmost sheet of the mass, that where hardly a light had twinkled or moved, becomes now a sparkling field of rhythmic flashing points with trains of travelling sparks hurrying hither and thither. The brain is waking and with it the mind is returning. It is as if the Milky Way entered upon some cosmic dance. Swiftly the head-mass becomes an enchanted loom where millions of flashing shuttles weave a dissolving pattern, always a meaningful pattern though never an abiding one; a shifting harmony of subpatterns. Now as the waking body rouses, subpatterns of this great harmony of activity stretch down into the unlit tracks of the stalk-piece of the scheme. Strings of flashing

and traveling sparks engage the length of it. This means that
the body is up and rises to meet its waking day.

This cosmic dance of the Milky Way, this enchanted
loom where millions of shuttles weave a dissolving but
always meaningful pattern, is, for me, a beautiful paradigm of the mind of Henry James. It illuminates his
darkness; it illustrates his genius for parenthesis. It is a
mind with a *presence*, and observing it work, watching
the shifting harmony of its dissolving patterns, will evoke
in some readers a sense of beholding the universe expand.
A sense of awe, disinterested awe, of the sort that James
himself would have found congenial, the life-enhancing
awe revealed in Sherrington's description, is one of the
pleasures, infrequent but rewarding, available to the traveler in darkest James. For some it may lie in the auto-
biographies, where it is less fictionally dark than factually
dense, but where the shuttle of his memory is peculiarly
luminous.

The exile of James is usually seen as a personal
dilemma, however wide its implications, rather than the
forerunner of the exile state of mind, the decade of
exodus that reached its climax in the twenties. But I
believe it was the *nature* of his exile to anticipate the
future: both the future of the novel and the predicament
of the novelist.

We continue to dwell on the exile of James rather than
on the meaning of his exile, or we would grasp that

through it he came into possession of his inheritance. No judgment we have rendered so exhibits what he described as our infantile lines of appreciation as this continued discussion of his questionable Americanism. In *The American Scene*, as I hope to demonstrate, he took possession of more of America, of both its past and its future, than the combined talents of those who are usually pushed forward to embarrass him. All of the evidence is in the book, and the book grew out of his exile; that is, out of his example.

In a world of diminishing raw material—the world that James inherited—it is James, virtually alone, who faced the crisis of the modern imagination. It is James, alone, who reversed the prevailing American tendency. If it was his fate to be gifted in such a way that he was isolated from his public, that is one of the facts, one of the many, that he would bid us face. That sturdy Anglo-Saxon gift for *knowing* the facts but refusing to admit what we know is one that he observed on both sides of the Atlantic. One of the functions of his novels was to make that admission possible—possible, but never compulsive. And the breadth and tolerance of his mind, the sanity and sweetness of his persuasion are nowhere so evident as when he is discussing his craft.

There is to my sense [he observed] no work of literary, or of any other, art, that any human being is under the smallest positive obligation to "like."

We can best understand the character of this statement if we turn to T. S. Eliot's remarks on James as a critic.

Even in handling men whom he could, one supposes, have carved joint from joint—Emerson, or Norton—his touch is uncertain; there is a desire to be generous, or a political motive, an admission (in dealing with American writers) that under the circumstances this was the best possible, or that it has fine qualities. . . . Henry was not a literary critic.

Mr. Eliot, who is a literary critic, one not adverse to carving adversaries joint from joint, here gives us an insight into the craft of the critic, and Henry's lack of it. It is this generosity—not his political motives—that gives to James's criticism what we find in his fiction: a life-enhancing rather than a life-debunking vitality. Without troubling to carve up either Emerson or Norton, he made, in his Prefaces and essays, observations on the novel that mark where modern criticism begins. It began, it is worth pointing out, in his genius and through his generosity.

The fallible James, the all-too-human James, the disquietingly artificial James are revealed through the seams in his *haut monde* façade. Small things, indeed the smallest things—the use of French to season both his fiction and his letters—reveal the native who is all too aware of his cultural impoverishment. In spite of the elegance of his prose and its apparent ease in the *salon* situation, these gems of culture, rubbed bright as a penny, are obviously foreign to it. They are worn for display, and differ in degree but not in kind from Whitman's *Libertad,* his occasional *trottoir* and his old *feuillage.*

This habit casts a disturbingly artificial shade over those moments when James, alone with his genius, speaks to it and to himself. The *mon bon* is touching, the *causons, causons, mon bon* is poignant and moving, but the question might be asked whether James, alone with his genius, was sufficiently alone. The shade of a cultural lag is there, self-consciously nudging him. A darker shade, the substance, we might say, of what both inspired and haunted him, is also manifest in this relationship. *Mon bon* is all there is. In this greeting are both his genius and his life. *Causons, causons, mon bon* is a call for a sign, a further proof, a further reassurance, of the sanctity and sufficiency of his life in art. What matters is the sign itself. Where the genius is sufficient, the sign is forthcoming, and James is such testimony as we need that a life, a great life, in and through art is possible. All that one needs is his genius, his devotion, and, for the fainthearted, his example.

The strange case of James and the theater is less strange if seen as a grand and fatal passion. His life, his life and his work, called for one. The theatrical Muse, more than the masculine novel, would exercise this passionate side of his nature—his so-called wooing of the public part of the trappings of the romance. Passion

notably blinds men, and the blindness of James to the
nature of his plays testifies to one of the great blind passions of his age. In the novel his uniqueness was tolerated
—in so many misleading ways they looked like novels—
but there is no way, on the stage, of dramatizing *consciousness*. There may come to be, but it was not James's
gift to discover it. The years he devoted to this experiment can best be understood as an *affaire du coeur*, an
almost scandalous pursuit of a notorious beauty by a mid-
dle-aged man. "Sublimation"—one of the many facts that
James turned to the advantage of his genius—afforded
him, in the theater, a public display of his one and only
passion—his dedication to the Muse. There is no doubt
he felt, at the time, that her favors were eluding him.
The theater was the way both to rekindle his passion and
to attract the lady's fading attentions. The *incident* of
Guy Domville, the spectacle of James, of all people,
suffering in such a manner, is harrowing in the tradition
of hopeless infatuation, of unrequited love. He came out
of it—as was his intention—a different man. Within the
next ten years, terminating in *The Golden Bowl*, his craft
and his consciousness continued to expand; magisterially,
at Rye, he performed the miracles after whose secrets
the avant-garde were groping. In the fullness of his
powers he returned to America. In *The American Scene*
we have his report. It shows him in full possession of
more of his native land than any figure since Tocqueville,

whose insights into the spirit of the place he both expands and supplements. The American Scene was finally seen and possessed by an American.

Fifty years before the lost generation went abroad to find themselves, James began his lonely pilgrimage. The exiles of the twenties, running in herds and sustained by the pack, had only to follow the call of the wild and indulge in it. The rediscovery of America came later, as a hangover. James ran with the fashionable pack, like the rest he toured, dined, and ogled, very much like the rest, and his early *vibrations* hardly differed, in kind, from those that were fashionable. If it had not been for the scandal of *Daisy Miller*—that "outrage to American girl-hood"—his fashionable period might have endured for some time. But there is reason to believe that his exile, his true *dis*patriation, began at that point. It made the act of repossession both necessary and possible. The exile of James, so far from being an unfortunate evidence of his sensibility, was the method through which he rediscovered America. The proof of this lies in the grain of his works, and for those who found this grain too fine he took the trouble to spell it out, with singular emphasis, in *The American Scene*. Few exiles, and even fewer natives, came to terms with this book. Published at the time when Mark Twain was lost in the despair of *What is Man?*, it would have given him a clue to that question, and one even more inscrutable—the one asked by Crèvecoeur a century earlier, "what is an American?" No one in America, or in England, for that matter, would have thought of turning to James for an answer. But the essential materials for an answer lie in his book. Such a query would have amused him, but on the evidence, and through his example, he is the first to inform us that to be an American is not enough. There is more to be said, and he said it, for human consciousness.

The gratifying sentiment that a man of genius is either lifting us up or speaking with our voice is one of the many clichés not applicable to James. He has his own voice. He seldom alters its pitch. As it drones on, interminably, the shuttle of his consciousness leaving nothing unconscious, he first puts us all to shame, then, as a rule, to sleep. He is, he may perhaps always be, too much for us. If we ask what in the world he is talking about, the only sensible rejoinder is the world of Henry James, that *new universe* of James, which we can see expanding as we gaze at it, a segment of the Milky Way, a nebula, engaged in its cosmic dance.

The formidable genius of James did not find its resolution in the novel. The form peculiar to his gifts emerged too late. His talents called for technical innovations as novel as those of Joyce and Proust, but he was content, on the whole, to pour his wine into old bottles. It is this that lies at the root of the perennial question of Henry James.

In James there are no Karamazovs, no Emma Bovarys,

there are no Swann's Ways, Whale's ways, or Huckleberry Finns. There is no *space*, as there is in Tolstoi,
there is no *place*, as there is in Hardy, and it is a mistake
to look for them. What, then, is there? There is parenthesis. The subject of James's appalling technique was
neither people nor places, things nor situations, but
the nature, the creation, of consciousness—to be totally
conscious, to be *one on whom nothing is lost.*

This seemed merely inspired common sense when he
advised it, but its relentless practice exposed him to madness, to the violence and chaos of a world dissolving, to
the feeling of horror that is prophetically modern in *The
Golden Bowl*. It exposed him to the acid bath of the
destructive element.

To have to take it all now [he wrote in 1915] for what the
treacherous years were all the while really making for and
meaning, is too tragic for any words.

So it was, but the "treacherous years" would serve as a
title for the years of the modern: it is the climate, the
atmosphere, the very air that the artist must breathe—in
particular that artist on whom nothing is lost.

"Too tragic for any words"—and yet only words, for
the writer, will come to terms with it. It is this that
explains—wherever such an explanation is necessary—the
modern artist's life in his art, and the nature of its self-

sufficiency. In reference to Joyce and *Ulysses*, T. S. Eliot observed:

In using the myth, in manipulating a continuous parallel between contemporaneity and antiquity, Mr. Joyce is pursuing a method which others must pursue after him. . . . It is simply a way of controlling, of ordering, of giving a shape and a significance to the immense panorama of futility and anarchy which is contemporary history.

Henry James is the bridge between the past that made sense, the real past, and the present that does not. He lived to expose himself to this fact, to full awareness of it. He was the first American of unquestioned genius to escape from the consolations of the past, without recourse to the endless vistas of optimism. Caught between the past and the future, immersed to the eyes in the destructive element, he remained true to his genius—one on whom nothing, no, *nothing*, was lost.

EIGHT

ABUSE OF THE PAST

NORMAN ROCKWELL

When we think of Don Quixote most of us will visualize the lean seedy figure in the pen drawings of Doré, an erect spindly wraith, seated on his bony nag, followed by the slouched, melancholy Sancho. If the pan is on his head it seems a small detail, just another crazy part of a witless old man. We see him spear in hand, we see him tilting windmills, we see him thrown from his ridiculous horse, but I think we never see him as he wished to see himself —*invisible*. He is all too visible, and in every inch mad as a coot. The element of humor in it appeals to us, but the element of wonder, I'm afraid, escapes. The golden Helmet of Mambrino is a piece of nonsense. We are all Sanchos at heart.

If we now conjure up the picture I have in mind, it will be a new one. Let us imagine Don Quixote, crowned with the battered barber's basin, attended by his ever-faithful Sancho, as he would appear on a cover of the *Saturday Evening Post*, as he would appear through the eyes and technique of Norman Rockwell.

I doubt that such an illustration exists, but I think that most Americans, at the suggestion, could supply it: a very lifelike figure—resembling somebody we know, a neighbor or a member of the family—on a horse that we had seen that morning, drawing the milk cart, wearing the basin in which we had, as a boy, washed our feet. I am not invoking this picture to ridicule it. Quite the contrary, since if we hope to understand the "imagination in America" we must start, if not end, with this master of verisimilitude, with this artist who, above all others, *heightens* the appearance of reality.

In speaking of the future of the novel James said: "Beginnings, as we all know, are usually small things, but continuations are not always strikingly great ones. . . ." In the beginning was Norman Rockwell. The continuations have not been strikingly great. From such a fact there is more to be gleaned than the usual sophisticated despair, or ironic amusement.

We can say, first, last, and always, that Norman Rockwell has been true to his beginnings, to his trust in his own and American sentiment. He is a genre painter; he uses graphic means to tell a story. His technique may be described as the most perfect where it dissolves, imperceptibly, into anecdote. This anecdotal picture that tells a simple story is the father of the story that gives us the simple picture, the *same* picture, as a rule—an unadorned, unpretentious, photographically convincing portrayal of *real* life.

In a period of forty years Rockwell has supplied the *Post* with more than three hundred of its covers. He has taught a generation of Americans to see. They look about them and see, almost everywhere they look, what Norman Rockwell sees—the tomboy with the black eye in the doctor's waiting room; the father discussing the Facts of Life with his teen-age son; the youth in the dining car on his first solo flight from home; and the family in the car, headed for an outing, followed by the same family on the tired ride home.

The convincing *realism* of the details, photographic in its accuracy, is all subtly processed through a filter of sentiment. It is this sentiment that heightens the reality, making it, for some, an object of affection, for others— a small minority—an object of ridicule. It all depends on that intangible thing the point of view.

Countless young men and women at the beginning of careers in art, have tried, and usually failed, to explain *their* point of view to a puzzled mother, a skeptical father. What can be wrong—Father would like to know —with Norman Rockwell, who is so obviously *good*? The answer is his very *goodness*, of course, but this usually ends the argument. Discussion leads nowhere. The two points of view go their different ways.

After considerable exposure to "modern" art, in museums, fashion magazines, the world of advertising, and everyday living, that mythic figure, the man in the street, will still go along with Norman Rockwell. And so—

whenever they can get him—will the *Saturday Evening Post*. In that respect, the times have not changed. A vote for Norman Rockwell is a vote for the *real* America. It is the nature of his gift that his very technique appears to dissolve into the subject, leaving the deposit of sentiment we like, otherwise no trace. After we have recognized the figures as our neighbors, and the street they live on as our own, we are left precisely where we came in—at the beginning. It is the nature of the genre piece to limit itself to clichés.

But if this charge is leveled at Norman Rockwell, it is leveled in suspension and will never reach him. Norman Rockwell is not there. In the picture we attack there is only ourselves. This is why such an attack gets us fighting mad. That row of photographs we keep on the piano has been maligned. However, this will help to explain the almost total absence of transitional material between Grant Wood's "Iowa Gothic"—which is true to the Rockwell tradition—and the sort of painting that most young people are doing today. It was easier to leap directly into the arms of God or the Devil than fight across the no man's land of raw-material clichés. A clean break—on such a battlefield—was the only one possible.

The extent to which this gap remains—and will continue to remain, we can feel with assurance—is evident in Rockwell's painting of Jennifer Jones in *The Song of Bernadette*. When the movie was released, Twentieth Century-Fox turned to Norman Rockwell, the illustrator, rather than to the resources of the movie camera, to portray and advertise the star in the leading role. That the movie industry should choose Norman Rockwell is both a testimony to his craft and a revealing commentary on the prevailing American taste. Our *realistic* front still has its soft, yellow-filter sky.

A more recent example, in the form of a tribute, were Rockwell's portraits of the Presidential candidates. It was left to Rockwell, in this sense, to reveal what the camera angles concealed, and to give the people—insofar as they were self-evident—the facts. Mr. Rockwell's Stevenson is the most instructive: we see the wit and intellectual cut down to our size, not cut down with malice, but, rather, with affection, as the neighbors of a "famous" man know him to be a simple, regular guy. Mr. Stevenson emerges as the man we usually find behind a drug counter, shrewd in his way, of independent mind, and willing to both take and give advice. He is one of us, not at all the sort of egghead we had heard about.

Scrutinized, held under the light that we find the most illuminating—the soft-sharp lens of Rockwell's craft— our raw material is seldom raw at all. It is hardly material. The clinical word for it is cliché. In the beginning, this credo reads, was the cliché. The raw-material effect is like the tinseled snow hung on the rootless trees at Christmas, stimulating the sensation without the embarrassment of the facts.

The paradox of our situation might be put like this:

having either exhausted, or depleted, the raw material that appeals to us, we needed a technician to create the illusion that it was still there. Rockwell is that technician. He understands the hunger, and he supplies the nourishment. The hunger is for the Good Old Days—the black-eyed tomboy, the hopeless, lovable pup, the freckled-faced young swain on his first date, the kid with white flannels at his first prom—sensations we no longer have, but still seem to want, dreams of innocence, as a rule, before they became corrupt.

This entire genre world, crowded with the artifacts that give it pathos and conviction, is generally inhabited by children, friendly animals, loving mothers, and wise old ladies and gentlemen. The beginnings of life come in for sentimental comment—often touching and pene-trating—the Huckleberry Finn myth of our lost youth, the territory of dreams that always lay ahead. But what that territory turned out to really *be*, neither Mark Twain nor Rockwell will tell us. It is a world of onsets, maiden speeches, first blushes, first impressions, and new departures; a universe of firsts: first dog, first kiss, first heartbreak, and first love. At the end of this journey, somehow sweetened by a life that has evaded both reali-zation and comment, we find the very old engaged in prayer, dozing with kittens, tolerating youngsters, or humorously caught in one of the innocent traps of life: a barber chair, a rumble seat, a train coach shared by a pair of young lovers, or a bench where the squirrels rifle our pockets while we sleep.

Between our first love, which is implicitly our last, and our last nap, which is implicitly forever, there is very little. What there is can be summed up in a word. *It's a joke, son.* In what is perhaps his most revealing work—one in which he portrays his full range of types—Rockwell illustrates the joke in question making its rounds. Here is *la ronde*, the permissible *ronde* American. It is clear that a good joke is something that good Americans can exchange. The democratic process can be seen at work as this joke makes its rounds from man to man, woman to woman, level to level, until it finally comes full circle—back, that is, to the man on whom the joke was played. They are all, needless to say, *good* American types. The democratic process is also at work, since we see no black men, no yellow men, no obvious Jews, Italians, or roughnecks—just plain folks, one of us. What the joke is we can almost guess. It is one that is funny to all these people. And it goes without saying that it is not *dirty*, though it might have an edge. It is basically good-hearted, basically good clean fun.

This interlude between first love and last breath is an illustrated version of Old Macdonald, forever down on his farm, where funny things are forever happening. Sex raises its adolescent murmur, not its ugly head. In this panel of profiles, this great family portrait, Rockwell

gives us the long span of a lifetime between the first and
the last joke we have heard. In this report, consciously
or otherwise, a note of comment can be detected that is
usually conspicuously absent from his work. His people
are always, we might say, *comfortably* real. But in this
portrait they verge on the uncomfortable. The raw material is so raw it almost speaks for itself. The effect—
the cumulative effect, since we deal here with a group
portrait—is something more than the sum of its parts.
If the eye remains on the page, and slowly follows the
joke through all of its phases, a disquieting, nonhumor-
ous impression builds up. How does it happen? It is clear
that they are all just goodhearted folks. But it is also
clear, increasingly, that they have nothing else on their
minds, that until the joke came along they had nothing
else to *exchange*. It is the joke that binds them together
in brotherhood. Missing from this tableau is the dirty-
minded lowbrow who would have spoiled all the fun, and
the egghead who might have used it for his own ends.
The joke comes full circle pretty much as it was told.

In a series of 1957 calendar illustrations, entitled "The
Four Seasons," Mr. Rockwell supplies us with a credo
that lucidly sums up his function as an artist. This is his
statement:

In a world that puts such importance on the pursuit of youth, it
is good to consider, occasionally, the charms—and the comforts—
of maturity. For whatever else may be said, maturity fosters

familiarity which in turn gives feelings of security and understanding that are valuable in these days of continuing change. I have tried to show these feelings in the paintings for the new Four Seasons calendar.

My pictures show two people who, after living together for many years, have reached the stage of sympathy and compatibility for which all of us strive. They know their weaknesses and their strengths. They are comfortable and secure in their relationships with each other. And while Mother presumably takes Father's strong points for granted, she's still trying tolerantly to keep him on the straight and narrow when signs of frailty appear.

Paintings like these are fun to do. While they are humorous, they are also human, and the subtle touch of forbearance evident in each of them is something all of us can learn. I can only hope you'll enjoy looking at these pictures as much as I have enjoyed working on them.

Perhaps the reader can visualize the "subtle touch of forbearance" in these illustrations. It verges closely—in the words of a recent parody in *Punch*—on the Brighter Side of the Bubonic Plague. Maturity—whatever else may be said—seen through the forbearance of Mr. Rockwell seems to be an adolescent pipe dream of the genial aspects of senility. The pursuit of youth is made more visible, rather than less, in these gentle fuddy-duddies, Mom and Pop, and their pathetic inability to grow *up*. A certain aging has taken place, but such growth as we

observe is downward and backward. That Mother takes
Father's strong points for granted is obvious, desperately
so—because Father's *strong* points are touchingly invisible. A genial pathos, sentimentally evoked, would seem
to be the mortar that binds them together, and provides
the comfort in what we describe as their "relationship."
That hard-work marriage has given way to the slogans
inscribed on the insurance posters, where the happy smiling couple are preserved, safe from *old* age, in the amber
of leisure. Nothing will touch them but the postman, with
his monthly retirement check.

All of the durable clichés we have already described
are served up afresh in these four tableaux. "Winter"
shows us the calendar being nailed to the wall, one that
features a pin-up girl discreetly censored—not the sort
of tempting dish that men or boys, if the distinction
exists, pin up for real delectation. "Spring" finds Father
down with a cold, lovingly wrapped up in Mother's
patchwork quilt, his feet in a pan of water as she spoon-
feeds him what is so obviously good for him. "Summer"
finds him in the yard, in a state of collapse, after a tussle
with the lawn mower, while Mother, with a compassion-
ate gaze, stands waiting to pour him a glass of lemonade.
In all these pictures a cat, symbol of the loving home,
is conspicuously evident, and proves, in his kittenish
ways, to be as young in heart as his masters.

The date beneath these illustrations is 1957—but they

are daydreams from a timeless past: only Mother's somewhat battered leather moccasins indicate that the time is
the present. Immortal moths escape from the holes in
Father's pair of red flannels, indicating that with "Au-
tumn" something called Winter is near. The mature
round of life—American style—in this manner comes
full cycle, leaving the reader prepared and expectant
for the new calendar that will usher in the New Year.
We are free to rest assured that Mother will keep Father
on the straight and narrow path.

We might say that Mr. Rockwell's special triumph is
in the conviction his countrymen share that this mythic
world he evokes actually exists. This cloudland of nostalgia seems to loom higher on the horizon, as the horizon
itself, the world of actual experience, disappears from
view. The mind *soars off*—in the manner that highways,
with new model cars, soar off into the future—leaving
the drab world of commonplace facts and sensations behind. In soaring into the past, rather than the future,
Mr. Rockwell is true to himself and his public, since that
is where the true territory ahead actually lies. In knowing
this he illustrates, with admirable fidelity, the American
Land of Heart's Desire.

If we now return to our imaginary painting, Mr. Rockwell's conception of Don Quixote, the pathetic old man,
with the brass basin on his head, in the charge of the
shrewd but loyal Sancho, we will sense to what extent he

will reveal more than the obvious humor of it. There would be a touch of pity, a touch of pathos, and a quantity of good-humored affection—but of wonder, that transforming element, not a drop. He is a childish old man with bats loose in his belfry—not unlike one we have in the family—and we identify ourselves with Sancho, rather than with him, with poor old Sancho, who, like ourselves, has to humor him. As for that helmet on his head, it is plainly a barber's basin. We all know that. We are Sanchos to the core, and he speaks with our voice when he cries that he can no longer bear in patience the wind and the lies, the buggery and humbuggery that the old man gives out. There is pity for an old fool, humor for a young one, and between the two of them, a joke, a good, clean joke.

Pathos—the only serious sentiment we will permit ourselves, without embarrassment—might reveal itself unconsciously in this portrait, as a touch of malice revealed itself in "The Joke." Rockwell plainly knows, as he assumes we do, that the dream is in the past. The Great Good Place is back there at the beginning, where it has always been. The faces in "The Joke," all meant to be contemporaries, have the cracker-barrel look of period pieces, *characters* in the sense that time will no longer alter them. Many of these people are Rockwell's Yankee neighbors—or reasonable facsimiles of them—but they are selected for what they represent, and they represent the past. The present exists, if at all in Rockwell, as a frame that heightens the nostalgia—the doctor's crisp waiting room where the tomboy with her black eye smilingly waits.

How many American fathers—if not mothers—would like to have had a girl like *that*, not like the jitterbugging, all-too-sex-conscious little number he has, not like the present, that is, but more like the imagined past.

In "Thanksgiving, 1951"—one of the most successful of his *Post* covers—Rockwell portrays an old lady and a small boy, the permissible extremes of our awareness, seated at a table in a "rough" railroad restaurant, saying grace. The youths and elderly men who surround them are all touchingly aware, and properly *touched*. The central figures, the old lady and the boy, have been lifted from some genre piece of the past, lock, stock, and barrel, and show no taint of existing in the world where we find them. The boy wears what such little boys were wearing during World War I. The old lady has her alligator bag, her umbrella, and her sewing reticule on the floor at her side. No cliché has been evaded. Every cliché is treated with the utmost respect. Through the window a modern locomotive steams in the yard.

How times have changed! we exclaim, and see our *self* as that pious unspoiled boy, and this fragment of the past as the real past that is gone.

But these characters appear out of neither the past nor

the hidden byways of the present, but, rather, out of the thin air of our imaginative need for them. That tomboy, with her blackened eye, and that puzzled teen-ager getting the Facts of Life, are meticulously illustrated daydreams to put the sad daily facts out of mind. These fantasies, generated on the trains whisking urban fathers to their homes in the suburbs, are meant to be fictions, lacking any connection to real life. It was in the past— just yesterday, that is—that there were giants in the earth, dreams in our hearts, love in our homes, religion in our churches, honor in our markets, and a future of such promise that the very thought of it brings an ache to the throat, and the eyes grow dim. In youth and age— a hopeful look forward or a yearning glance backward—Rockwell sustains the sentimental extremities of our lives. In between, making its eternal round, filling up the big central gap in our existence, is the joke. Stop me if you've heard this one, says the joker—but of course nobody does. After all, what else is there? *La ronde* is *le rire*.

If we now return to our imagined Don Quixote, the relationship between technique and raw material is made clear. The raw material is what counts. Technique is the way we gloss or heighten it with sentiment.

"Do you know what I think, Sancho?" said Don Quixote. "I think that this famous piece of that enchanted helmet must by some strange accident have fallen into the hands of someone who did not know, and was incapable of estimating, its worth, and who, seeing that it was of the purest gold and not realizing what he was doing, must have melted down the other half for what he could get for it, while from the remaining portion he fashioned what appears, as you have said, to be a barber's basin."

Having melted down the other half, from the remaining portion Rockwell has fashioned what appears to be a barber's basin. It is the basin as *basin* that interests us, and no transformation is desired. Such magical properties as it might possess transport us into the past, rather than into the future. It is the key, the Open Sesame, to our nostalgia. The battered basin, the bony nag, the old man with the bats loose in his belfry, are so many strings around our memory fingers, the unbroken ties we retain with the past. They transport us, rather than transform us, and it is the past, not the future, that beckons.

The element of folk wisdom in this pattern generates much that is good in our writing, but we are apt to overlook the crippling power of the cliché. The Helmet of Mambrino, shorn of its magic, hangs affectionately on that nail in the kitchen—because it is a basin, an *old* basin, not because it has unusual properties. It does not change us so much as remind us—what we want is not change but reminiscence—and, needless to say, what we want is what we get.

Among our many native gifts, which are large, is one that is seldom singled out for comment. It is the faculty, one might say the intuition, we have by which we trans-

form adult works of art, few as they are, into children's
books. We transform them into books that are *safe*. *Moby
Dick* and *Huckleberry Finn* are not merely safe for boys
to read, but are even read by them. They are adventure
stories, on the shelf with *Treasure Island* and *Tom Swift*.
It would seem to be here, and here alone, that the transforming powers of the Helmet of Mambrino are part of
our tradition. We transform the adult into a child. It is
the converse of transforming the present into the past.
In either case we get back to the beginnings, back to the
innocence before it was corrupted, back to that time when
the world and ourselves were young.

A boy's-eye view of the world, enchanted in *Tom Sawyer*, disenchanted in *Huckleberry Finn*, is wonderfully
blended in the art of Norman Rockwell and seasoned to
taste. Here we can often have it both ways. The grown-up
world impinges on the past only to heighten its flavor,
the purity of the enchantment, the sweet pathos of the
light that failed. Old folks—people who once again are
notoriously childlike—reappear to reaffirm, in their seasoned wisdom, the youthful dreams. At the extremities
of our life, two aspects of the childlike meet. It is the
childish dream—somewhat battered by the interlude of
life—that once again, in its wisdom, dominates our lives.
An old man's gnarled hand, one finger clutched by a boy's
small hand, sums it all up. The beginning and the ending
of the dream are thus made one.

Mark Twain, the one who didn't like books, would have seen eye to eye with Norman Rockwell, since it is Twain's eyes through which Rockwell customarily sees. It is the world of Tom Sawyer, Huck Finn, and Aunt Sally brought up to date. It is still the old battle of Aunt Sally and her civilizing ways, all of it under the watchful eyes of grownups who are still—bless their hearts—children at heart themselves. They have grown up, but we have no idea how they got that way. They are included in the picture to frame and heighten what came *first*. Childhood came first, of course, and young dreams, and all those promises that men fail to live by— but back then they were real, back *then* we believed in them. Whereas, if you look around you now—but of course we don't. *It's a joke, son.* It's much better to look, as we do, into the mythic past.

A world of beginnings, of exemplary firsts, is what we find, in various formations, in the works of Wolfe, Hemingway, Fitzgerald, and Faulkner. Their work spans, oddly enough, the period between Rockwell's first *Post* cover and his last. The battle is still the same old battle of Aunt Sally and her civilizing ways. It is nostalgia, in one form or another, that challenges the ability of each writer to function, as it determined the style and substance of Rockwell's craft. Here in America we begin, and occasionally we end, with the abuses of the past.

Part Four

THE ABILITY

TO FUNCTION

NINE

THE FUNCTION OF STYLE

ERNEST HEMINGWAY

Before I go on with this short history, let me make a general observation—the test of a first-rate intelligence is the ability to hold two opposed ideas in the mind at the same time, and still retain the ability to function. One should, for example, be able to see that things are hopeless and yet be determined to make them otherwise.   —F. Scott Fitzgerald, *The Crack-up*

"All modern literature," Hemingway stated in *The Green Hills of Africa,* "comes from one book by Mark Twain called *Huckleberry Finn."* In such a comment there is an uncanny amount of truth, but it is a characteristically revealing, oversimplified observation. What the master is saying is, "I began with Huckleberry Finn." It was perhaps inspired in order to settle the dust on that tiresome quarrel with Gertrude Stein—who claimed that she gave birth to Ernest—but, as he indicates, it was Twain who got in the first, and the *last* lick.

In the essentials, Ernest Hemingway, born in Illinois, is a latter-day Huckleberry Finn. His "Big Two-Hearted

River" is a latter-day retreat into the wilderness. The differences are precisely those that time would have made, what time would have done to both Huck and the territory ahead. He would have learned, at a very early age, that there was no such animal. His life would have begun with disenchantment rather than enchantment: he would be the first of that new breed of young men who knew too much, who knew more than their fathers would admit to knowing.

The boy who witnessed the death in the Michigan woods came out of the woods a man no longer subject to change. He had had it. But it took time to learn *what* he had had. The nature of this disenchantment is described with classic finality in the stories and sketches of *In Our Time*. The man who emerged lived and wrote by the values forged in his fiction. Both the writer and his work, that is, resisted change. A process of "seasoning," rather than development, links the disillusion of *In Our Time* with the resolution of *The Old Man and the Sea*. The facts are the same. You can't win. In the long run, life will beat you. First the big fish eat the little ones, then the little fish eat the big ones. But a brave and simple man can win a bit of the laurel, nevertheless. In never giving up, win or lose, he enjoys a final triumph over death itself.

With this wisdom, dramatized in a tale that is a lucid model of his craft, few modern men will care to argue. It seems true to life, and we know it is true to Hemingway. It is what he has been saying, and how he has been living, since he stepped, just forty years ago, to the edge of the wilderness and did not like at all what he saw. To that shock of recognition he has been consistent. In his life and his art he has been his own man. His craft has cast a spell that both inspires and takes a yearly toll. In attempting to come to terms with this man—or, as I choose to believe, this *style*—we are essentially concerned with coming to terms with his age, with the fact that he is largely responsible for it. His style—like the clear water that flows at the heart of all of his fiction—sounds the note of enchantment to the very disenchantment it antici-pates. The reader grasps, immediately, that this man is not so tough as he looks. Quite the contrary, he looks and sounds so tough because his heart is so soft. Behind the armor of his prose, the shell of his exile, lurks our old friend Huck Finn, American dreamer, the clean-cut boy who just wishes Aunt Sally would leave him alone, who wants nothing more, nor less, than a clearing of his own in the wilderness. The dream itself he left unchanged, he merely moved to a smaller river, but he brought to it a style that revealed the dream to itself. There was no need to cry "O lost, lost—lost!" in the voice of Tom Wolfe, since the style had absorbed the state of disenchantment: the style was it. It was not merely the man, nor a handful of crafty exiles, but the age itself, the old moon of enchantment with the new moon of disenchantment in its arms.

When the young man Hemingway came to the edge of the clearing, when he saw what man had left in the place of nature, he found it something more than an unpleasant shock. He found it unacceptable. In that early judgment he has never wavered. It is expressed with finality in his exile. In this feeling, and in his exile, he is not alone, but being an artist he has been able to give his judgment a singular permanence. As the style of Faulkner grew out of his rage—out of the impotence of his rage—the style of Hemingway grew out of the depth and nuance of his disenchantment. Only a man who had believed, with a child's purity of faith, in some haunting dream of life, in its vistas of promise, is capable of forging his disillusion into a work of art. It is love of life that Hemingway's judgment of life reveals. Between the lines of his prose, between the passage and the reader, there is often that far sound of running water, a pine-scented breeze that blows from a cleaner and finer world. It is this air that makes the sight of so many corpses bearable. Invariably it is there—a higher order than the one we see before us in operation—as if the legend of the past were stamped, like a signature, on his brow. We have never had a more resolute moralist. A dream of the good life haunts the scene of all the bad life he so memorably observes, and when under his spell it is the dream of the good life that we possess. For such an artist, should there be anything but praise? Could there be anything conceivably impotent about such a style? It is when we come to brood on his consistency—on the man who does not change, or seem aware of it—that we see that the author, as well as the reader, has been under a spell, the same spell—the spell of a style. The consistency lies in what the style will permit him to think, to feel, and to say.

Every writer who is sufficiently self-aware to know what he is doing, and how he does it, sooner or later is confronted with the *dictates* of style. If he *has* a style, it is the style that dictates what he says. *What* he says, of course, is *how* he says it, and when we say that the style is the man we have testified to this property. The writer who develops, as a man and a writer, cannot be self-contained in a style, however memorable and charming, that has served its purpose. The style must change, or the writer must adapt himself to it. This is notably true of the writers whose style is the most highly personalized, and distinctive: the most distinctive stylist of this order in our time is Hemingway. He *is* a style. He has never departed from it. Tentative departures—in *For Whom the Bell Tolls*, for example—have appeared as flaws in the marble, rather than as symptoms of development. It is the nature of Hemingway's style to prohibit development. When he remains within it, he sounds *like himself*. When he attempts to escape, we do not know what he sounds like. Neither does he. It is a lesson he has taken to heart. *The Old Man and the Sea* is a two-way fable, that of an old man who has mastered a fish, and that of an aging writer who bows to the mastery of his style. Within these stylistic commitments he sounds all right. He does *not* sound, however, like he did more than thirty years earlier, when this style, and these commitments, were being forged. *The Old Man and the Sea* is an act of will; within the terms of this will it is a moving achievement, but as an act of the imagination it is dead. The style, not the creative mind, dictates the range and nature of the experience, selects the cast, and determines what is permissible. Here again the Spanish language—the simplifying agent—is used to reduce the complexities, in the manner of that memorable night of love and conversation in the sleeping bag. This technique, on occasion, leads to revelation, but as a rule it is merely reduction. The apparent simplicity lies in the style, rather than in the nature of the material, but Hemingway takes pains to build up a consistently simple scene. Man, fish, and Joe DiMaggio are attuned to the demands of the simple epic; complexities, human complexities, are reduced to a minimum. Complicated types enter Hemingway's world only to lose their complications. Man must appear simple, subject to simple corruptions, so that NATURE, writ large, will appear complex. The restoration of Nature— the Nature undefiled of the "Big Two-Hearted River"—

would seem to be the passion behind Hemingway's reduction of man. It is why his disillusion, limited to man,
is still grained with hope. Man is a mess, but Nature will
prevail. It is the sea that triumphs, the sea and the sky
against which man's puny drama is enacted, but they are
not used, as in Hardy, to dwarf man to insignificance;
rather, they remind him, in the complex way Hemingway
will not permit his characters, of the paradise lost that
might still be regained, that green breast of the world
Huck Finn preserved in the territory ahead.

This scale of values—Man finitely simple, and Nature
infinitely complex—is the Hemingway palette and the
key to the scale of his style. He is never reduced to
tampering with personalities. A Cézanne-like simplicity
of scene is built up with the touches of a master, and the
great effects are achieved with a sublime economy. At
these moments style and substance are of one piece, each
growing from the other, and one cannot imagine that life
could exist except as described. We think only of what
is there, and not, as in the less successful moments, of all
of the elements of experience that are not.

The Hemingway economy, his sublime economy, is
one thing when dictated by the imagination, but another
when merely by the mechanical blue pencil of his style.
These two slices of life, superficially, will look the same.
Both will have the authority of his craft. There is no
litmus test that the reader can apply to distinguish be-

tween the prose, the economy of the prose, of *The Sun Also Rises* and *Across the River and into the Trees.* Both books are *written.* But only one has been creatively imagined. In the absence of the shaping imagination Hemingway can always rely on his *craft,* and he is one of the great craftsmen of the age. The proof of this, ironically enough, is less in the books that were intensely imagined than in the books that were primarily an act of will. Here it is craft, and craft alone, that sustains both the reader and the writer, and it is what we mean, what we feel to be true, in observing that the author has fallen under his own spell. Indeed he has. And the spell is almost enough. The response of a new generation to *The Old Man and the Sea* was evidence of how much an artist might achieve through pure technique.

This technique, this celebrated style, was born full-fledged—whatever the line of descent—and in nearly forty years it has undergone no visible change. Neither has the life it portrays, since the style and the slice of life are the same. In the interests of this style things remain as they are, they do not change. It is a lens of the finest precision; it records, accurately, the author's field of vision, but the price of the performance is that the *field* must remain the same. Time—in the sense of development—must stand still. The timeless quality of the Hemingway snapshot is truly timeless—growth and change have been removed. The illusion of things as they are is raised to a point that has seldom been equaled; a frieze-like sense of permanence enshrines the Big Two-Hearted River and its world-wide tributaries. This woodland stream, symbolic of all that is undefiled in both man and nature, rises at the source of Hemingway's young manhood and flows through his life and his work to the sea. Clear water, clear fast-moving water, links the exile, on a weekend in Spain, with the Big Two-Hearted River back in Michigan. From different streams the fisherman pulls the same trout. Good fish and running water serve him as the means of coming to terms with life.

As Thoreau went to Walden for the *facts*, Hemingway went to the Michigan woods and the bullfight. In the grain of both men was a passionate desire for reality—be it life or death. Both men feared only one thing: being cheated of life. The *big* cheat, for both men, was the world of Aunt Sally, and only in the woods could one see life cleanly, in the wilderness of nature, or, for Hemingway, in the *nature* of war. But one began in the wilderness.

He sat on the logs, smoking, drying in the sun, the sun warm on his back, the river shallow ahead entering the woods, curving into the woods, shallows, light glittering, big water-smooth rocks, cedars along the bank and white birches, the logs warm in the sun, smooth to sit on, without bark, gray to the touch; slowly the feeling of disappointment left him. It went away slowly, the feeling of disappointment that came sharply after the thrill that made his shoulders ache. It was all right now.

Any man who has ever tried to write will feel in this passage the line-taut passion of a man who would die rather than cheat you with a cliché. It is *this* that is moving—rather than what he tells us. We feel, in this prose, the man's passion for the truth. We hang on every word, as he intends, secure in the feeling that the word will support us. There is no thin ice in this style. We have our hands on experience. We are in possession of the facts.

On the Big Two-Hearted River the artist cut his teeth, but it is not till his exile that he clamps down with them. He waits, appropriately, till his exiles do a little fishing. It is in Spain, that the trout in the Big Two-Hearted River get their bite.

While I had him on, several trout had jumped at the falls. As soon as I baited up and dropped in again I hooked another and brought him in the same way. In a little while I had six. They were all about the same size. I laid them out, side by side, all their heads pointing the same way, and looked at them. They were beautifully colored and firm and hard from the cold water. It was a hot day, so I slit them all and shucked out the insides, gills and all, and tossed them over across the river. I took the trout ashore, washed them in the cold, smoothly heavy water above the dam, and then picked some ferns and packed them all in the bag, three trout on a layer of ferns, then another layer of ferns, then three more trout, and then covered them with ferns.

They looked nice in the ferns, and now the bag was bulky, and I put it in the shade of the tree.

This is like a summing up and a prophecy. After the sad goings on of the lost generation, we have plunged, in this stream, back to clean reality, beautifully colored and firm and hard, like the trout. That is nature. That is the nature of life. Bulls are sometimes good, sometimes bad, but only man is vile. In returning to nature it is possible for man to cleanse himself.

It is in keeping with this style that man should undergo a progressive brutalization, and nature a progressive refinement and serenity; that man, who should speak for himself, fails to do so, and that nature, who cannot, should become articulate. The river that flows through *The Sun Also Rises*, reflecting what is lost in the lost generation, is a clearer and more incorruptible stream than the one that flows through *In Our Time*. The Spanish stream has been *tested*. The trout are firm immortal trout. They lie before our eyes, all their heads pointing in the same direction, like the timeless fish in one of the paintings of Braque. Technique has snatched them from the river of life and made them into art.

The flowering of Hemingway's conception of life— and let us make no mistake, it is a conception—achieves its fullest expression in *Death in the Afternoon*. Although death is its subject, it is a book that teems with life. But

all of this life, with the exception of the eating and the
drinking, is life downgraded, reduced in scale to the ele-
mentary plane. The effect, however, is monumental—
like the figures in the drawings of Goya. Deprived of all
refinements, they loom with the starkness of some demonic force. It is nature that speaks, not the man himself.
We are in a scene virtually crammed with young men
who are nothing if not "eggheads"—but when this fact
appears in their thinking it is laughed out of court. In the
opening paragraph, that remarkable dictum that so well
describes the healthy bird of prey is given the power and
the sanction of Hemingway's style.

So far, about morals, I know only that what is moral is what
you feel good after and what is immoral is what you feel bad
after and judged by these moral standards, which I do not de-
fend, the bullfight is very moral to me because I feel very fine
while it is going on and have a feeling of life and death and
mortality and immortality and after it is over I feel very sad
but fine.

We need not concern ourselves with this as philosophy.
It is a remarkably accurate statement—with its built-in
escape clause—of a profoundly primitive state of being,
less human than subhuman, a voice of *laissez faire* from
the well of the past that would have frightened Nean-
derthal man. It is the first cry of that man who did not
want to be a man. He wanted his simple uncomplicated

feelings, his simple uncomplicated gratifications, and he did not want them troubled, at the time or later, by a lot of probing into *what* they were. He liked to eat, since after eating he felt good. He liked to make love—but not when it started getting complicated. He didn't mean to go so far as to say this was a good thing, since he liked it, but he did mean to say that at least he knew what he liked.

Now this statement grows, in my opinion, from the style more than it does from the man. It is the style that dictated the turn of the thought, and the style that gives it the ring of truth. Anything, in our time, *any*thing that cuts through the morass of talk and complications—that cuts through and gives light—understandably appeals to us. This sort of plain talk from the shoulder, when the shoulder is a good one, wins our attention. The frank admission and the manly qualification have been sorely abused since Hemingway set the fashion, but it is a fashion that is singularly American. In this voice, if not in these accents, speaks the spirit of Thoreau, Whitman, and Mark Twain. The American grain calls for plain talk, for the unvarnished truth. Better to err a little in the cause of bluntness than soften the mind with congenial drivel. Better a challenging half-truth than a discredited cliché.

The moralist in Hemingway, kept off stage in his fiction, comes to the footlights in *Death in the Afternoon* to shock the Old Lady with his "immoral" observations on life. What we have here is Huck Finn, grown a little older but not grown *up*, getting in a final lick, a last sassy word, on the subject of Aunt Sally. The style, here, serves him less well: it is the weapon of a bully rather than of an artist, wielded in the manner of his pronouncements on women, big-game hunting, and the press. However telling these pronouncements often are, they are chips from the rocks along the Big Two-Hearted River, and evidence that the man within the artist has not changed. He is still, like his master Mark Twain, a boy at heart. While we pause to read what he has to say he is already off for the territory ahead before the world, or Aunt Sally, tries to civilize him. He can't stand it.

THE FUNCTION OF

APPETITE

THOMAS WOLFE

Didn't Hemingway say this in effect: if Tom Wolfe ever learns to separate what he gets from books from what he gets from life, he will be an original.   —"Notebooks"

F. Scott Fitzgerald

If Tom Wolfe ever learned, he left no evidence of it. He never learned to separate what he got from books from what he got from life. His appetite wouldn't let him. A glutton for life, he actually died of impoverishment. He bolted both life and literature in such a manner he failed to get real nourishment from either. Nothing that he devoured, since it was not digested, satisfied his insatiable appetite. He was aware of that himself, and his now legendary hunger haunted him like the hound of heaven, and it became, in time, synonymous with life itself. *Appetite*. Slabs of raw life were reduced to crates of raw manuscript. The figure of Wolfe, a piece of manuscript in hand, standing beside a bulging crate of typewritten paper, convincingly symbolizes our raw-material myth and attests to our belief in it. Both the size of the man and the size of the crate are in *scale*.

No greater paradox could be imagined than this raw young giant, a glutton for life, whose experience, in substance, was essentially vicarious. He got it from books. He gives it back to us in books. His lyrical rhetoric and his sober narration—the full range, that is, of his style— derives from his reading, and his reading, like his living, was something he bolted.

If literature is your life—the artist's life—it, too, must be processed by your imagination. It must be transformed, as raw material is transformed, before it is possessed. In this transformation there is a destructive element. The artist must destroy, in this act of possession, a part of what he loves. In passing it on, through his own achievement, he leaves it different from what he found. It is the element of difference, not sameness, that testifies to his right of possession. But it is the element of sameness—transference rather than transformation—that we find in Wolfe. Described as the Walt Whitman of novelists, here is what he does, how he echoes Whitman:

Oh, there are women in the East—and new lands, morning, and a shining city! There are forgotten fume-flaws of bright

smoke above Manhattan, the forest of masts about the crowded
isle, the proud cleavages of departing ships, the soaring web, the
wing-like swoop and joy of the great bridge, and men with derby
hats who come across the bridge to greet us—come brothers, let
us go to find them all. For the huge murmur of the city's mil-
lion-footed life, far, bee-like, drowsy, strange as time, has come
to haunt our ears with all its golden prophecy of joy and triumph,
fortune, happiness, and love such as no men before have ever
known. Oh brothers . . .

This is meant to be an invocation. What we have is a
man with his eyes closed, his pores open, whipping himself into a state of intoxication with what is left of *another*
man's observations. The rhetorical flow, lyrical in intent,
is unable to keep up with the flow of the emotion, the
verbal surge of clichés, of scenic props, to the winded anticlimax of

the men with derby hats who come across the bridge to greet us
—come brothers, let us go to find them all.

The pathetic irrelevance of this touch is central to the
flow of fantasy. Rather than Whitman's artifacts, closely
and lovingly observed, we have a river of clichés, nouns
and soaring adjectives. This giant from the hills may be
in love with life, but he woos her with books. It is through
another man's eyes that he looks, and it is another man's
language that he uses. Life might well ask him, as
Priscilla did John Alden, to speak for himself. The
presence of raw material, real, raw, bleeding life—the

one thing that Wolfe believed he got his big hands on—
is precisely what is absent from his work. He begins and
he ends with raw-material clichés.

O youth, still wounded, living, feeling with a woe unutter-
able, still grieving with a grief intolerable, still thirsting with a
thirst unquenchable—where are we to seek? For the wild tempest
breaks above us. The wild fury beats about us, the wild hunger
feeds upon us—and we are houseless, doorless, unassuaged, and
drive on forever: and our brains are mad, our hearts are wild
and worldless, and we cannot speak.

This romantic agony, to put it charitably, is strictly
literary. He is choking on words in this passage, not on
raw life. In a letter to Fitzgerald—frequently cited to
show Wolfe's superior vitality and passion—Wolfe made
this confession:

. . . one of my besetting sins, whether you know it or not, is
lack of confidence in what I do.

It was a sound intuition. He *knew*, but he did not know
what he knew. It was a *feeling* he had, but like all of his
feelings it remained unexamined, one of his frequent
apprehensions, his premonitions of disorder and early
sorrow that increased, rather than calmed, his romantic
agony. In his effort to both release, and control his muse,
he had two styles. Samples of his "release," usually referred to as lyrical flights, I have quoted. In contrast to
the lyrical flight is sober, dispassionate, narrative.

It would have been evident to an observer that of the four people who were standing together at one end of the platform three—the two women and the boy—were connected by the relationship of blood.

This is "control." It is also unintentional parody. Max Beerbohm might have coined it to take care of the great *traditional* novel. Wolfe assumes the stance, he clears his throat, but the voice that issues from his mouth is not his own, and the words fall into unconscious parody. The shades of Thackeray and Trollope, in this prose, were not connected by the relationship of blood.

Periodically, as if purging ourselves of what we spend our lives making and doing, the American mind indulges in a hay ride—one climaxed with a bonfire and love among the haystacks—in order to remind ourselves that there is nobody like us. And indeed there is not. But we are insecure, as Wolfe was insecure, and never tire of the convincing reminder. The latest, but certainly not the last, was Thomas Wolfe. He came from the hills. He was six foot four and a man in every inch. He believed in doing nothing—as Faulkner reminds us—short of the impossible. The existence of the legend of Paul Bunyan may have given young Tom Wolfe something to shoot at, but in many ways he overshot the mark. The word prodigious—in energy, in scale, in talent, in ambition, and in failure—is the word that most happily character-

izes the pilgrimage. For Wolfe made one. He made one
for all of us. Although his song is a song of himself—a
choric forest murmur to the lyric Walt Whitman—his
hunger, insatiable as it was, was still too small. It is the
continent itself that seeks to speak in the bellow of Wolfe.
Everything observable, desirable, and, on certain rare
occasions, even conceivable is thrown into the hopper of
his hunger and—*bolted*. Nothing, absolutely *nothing*, is
left on the table. We see only where his elbows leaned,
and the crumbs he dropped.

What we observe in Wolfe—if we care to observe him
—is how a man *eats*. As we watch him eat his very appetite grows; he bolts his food, he reaches for more, and
in the very act of gorging himself he starves to death. It
is a vivid and appalling projection of our buried life. We
want to grasp life whole, grasp it raw and bleeding, and
then gulp it while it's hot. Sometimes we do. But the results are not what we were led to expect. Our appetite,
rather than being diminished, has increased. In living out
this dream of our buried lives—in living it up, as we
would now describe it—Wolfe threw himself into the
bonfire all of us had built. His identification with the
myth, with its attendant exaltations, and, as the fire began
to die, with the usual premonitions, took on the nature
of a public purge and sacrifice. These premonitions of
death are self-induced; an infinite craving finds its resolution in a craving for the infinite. In his prodigious effort,

in his prodigious failure, was our success. The prevailing tendency to start well, hewing a path, single-handed, through the wilderness around him, and then to fail, since to succeed is unheard of, is a credit to everyone. The highest honors, however, to Wolfe, the highest praise for his thinking that he could do it—but even higher honors to the unconquerable continent itself, to us, that is. We are simply too colossal, as Wolfe was too colossal himself.

When Thomas Wolfe died, at thirty-seven, it was said that had he lived he might have done it, might have grasped what still seemed to elude him, might have tamed the untamable, and in holding out such infinite hope for him, we hold it out for ourselves. It is the sentiment that both sustained and destroyed him—infinite hope, infinite yearning, infinite love, ambition, and hunger, into which the finite world of experience slowly dissolved. An infinite amount of nonraw material overwhelms a very finite fragment of craft, and his barbaric yawp drowned out every voice in the air but his own.

The continent too big for one man to tame it, the story too big for one man to tell it, the manuscript too big for one crate to hold it, one man to shape it—this myth of too-muchness received its classic affirmation in the figure of Wolfe. In identifying himself, lavishly, with the malady that masquerades as a virtue, he lived to the hilt the illusion that is fatal to both the man and the artist. The impotence of *material*, raw or otherwise, receives its

widest advertising in his mammoth showcase—almost
everything is there but the imagined thing, and all of it
bigger than life. The sight of all these objects generated
in Wolfe sentiments and sensations of a literary nature,
and on occasion, unknowingly, he was moved to something like creative activity. But *that* sensation, singularly
unfamiliar, and smacking unmistakably of *self*-control,
and self-denial, was the one sensation that he deeply distrusted, distrusted intuitively one might say. That sort of
thing led him away from *himself*, and where, if any-
where, did that lead?

He didn't know, and he put off, deliberately, every
chance to find out. His artistic solution was to write the
same book over and over again, each time in the hope
that this time the spirit would inhabit it, each time in the
hope that his chronic self-doubt would stop tormenting
him. The chorus of praise, world-wide, did not console
or beguile him. After all, he *knew*. He knew better than
those who hailed his failure as a success. As a martyr to
our greed, our insatiable lust for life, which makes life
itself an anticlimax, Wolfe is such proof as we need that
appetite and raw material are not enough. They are where
art begins, but to begin at all calls for the tools of technique.

Loneliness, as a theme of adolescence, rather than
aloneness, a condition of man, is what the reader finds in
Wolfe and what will assure his continued popularity. It

is idle to speak of Wolfe's defects as a writer, since it is precisely the defects that we find immortal. In them, on a cineramic scale, we see ourselves. Wolfe's impressive powers of description persuaded him, as it does most of his readers, that imaginative power of an impressive range was being exercised. On the evidence the contrary is the case, description takes the place of imagination, and an excess of description, a rhetoric of hyperbole, take the place of imaginative passion.

His book—for it is all one book—offers us the extraordinary spectacle, both haunting and appalling, of the artist as a cannibal. An insatiable hunger, like an insatiable desire, is not the sign of life, but of impotence. Impotence, indeed, is part of the romantic agony. If one desires what one cannot have, if one must do what cannot be done, the agony in the garden is one of self-induced impotence. It is Wolfe's tragic distinction to have suffered his agony for us all.

ELEVEN

THE FUNCTION OF

NOSTALGIA

F. SCOTT FITZGERALD

"Can't repeat the past?" he cried incredulously. "Why of course you can."   —Jay Gatsby

The "subject" of Wolfe, Hemingway, and Faulkner, however various the backgrounds, however contrasting the styles, pushed to its extremity, is nostalgia. But it was left to F. Scott Fitzgerald, the playboy, to carry this subject to its logical conclusion. In fictional terms this is achieved in *The Great Gatsby*. In personal terms it is achieved in *The Crack-up*.

Thomas Wolfe's nostalgia, his cry of *"Lost, lost, lost —"* was a cliché he neither transformed nor examined, but Fitzgerald made of it a form of consciousness. Nostalgia, quite simply, is *all* there is. In plumbing this sentiment to its depths, rather than merely using or abusing it, Fitzgerald dropped to the deep, dead-end center of the American mind. He let his line out deeper than Hemingway and Twain, deeper than the Mississippi and the Big-Two Hearted River, down to that sunken island that once mythically flowered for Dutch sailors' eyes.

That was where the dream began, he tells us, that still pandered to men in whispers: that was where man held his breath in the presence of this brave new world. It was Fitzgerald, dreaming of paradise, who was compelled to an aesthetic contemplation that made of nostalgia, that snare and delusion, a work of art.

Through all he said, even through his appalling sentimentality, I was reminded of something—an elusive rhythm, a fragment of lost words, that I had heard somewhere a long time ago. For a moment a phrase tried to take shape in my mouth and my lips parted like a dumb man's, as though there was more struggling upon them than a wisp of startled air. But they made no sound, and what I had almost remembered was uncommunicable, forever.

That elusive rhythm, that fragment of lost words, that ghostly rumble among the drums are now, thanks to Fitzgerald, a part of our inheritance. Those who were never there will now be there, in a sense more compelling than those who were there, since they will face it, and grasp it, in the lucid form of Fitzgerald's craft. Like Gatsby, he, too, believed in the green light, in the orgiastic future that recedes before us, leading by a strange circumambulation back into the past, back to those dark fields of the republic where the Big Two-Hearted River flows into the Mississippi, and the Mississippi flows, like time, into the territory ahead. Time and the river flow backward, ceaselessly, into the mythic past. Imperceptibly, the function of nostalgia reduces the ability to function.

The power and sources of nostalgia lie beyond the scalpel. Nostalgia sings in the blood, and with age it grows thicker, and when all other things fail it joins men in a singular brotherhood. Wherever they live in the present, or hope to live in the future, it is in the past that you will truly find them. In the past one is safely out of time but not out of mind.

Nostalgia is a limbo land, leading nowhere, where the artist can graze like a horse put to pasture, feeding on such clover of the past as whets the appetite. The persuasive charm of Fitzgerald is that this clover, which he cups in both hands, is almost chokingly sweet. We dip our faces into the past as into the corridor of that train, homeward bound at Christmas, the air scented with luggage, coonskin coats, and girls with snow melting in their hair. But it has a greater virtue still. It is inexhaustible. It is the artist—not the vein of nostalgia—that gives out or cracks up.

As a man steps from the wings of his own imagination

to face the music, the catcall facts of life, Fitzgerald
stepped forward in the *The Crack-up* to face the audience.
It is a *performance*. He knows the crowd is openly
snickering at him. For this curtain call, however, which
nobody asked for, an apologetic *apologia pro vita sua*, he
has reserved the few lines, implicit but unspoken, in his
books. Self-revelation as revealing as this, many found
contemptible. Not that he had cracked up—that was
commonplace—but that in cracking up he had owned
up to it. Nor would that have really mattered if, in own-
ing up, he hadn't owned anything. But Fitzgerald *knew*.
That was the hell of it. He was the first of his generation
to know that life was *absurd*.

It is fitting that Fitzgerald, the aesthete of nostalgia,
of the escape clause without question, should be the first
American to formulate his own philosophy of the absurd.
But nostalgia, carried to its conclusion, leads nowhere
else. Had he been of the temperament of Albert Camus,
he might have been the first to dramatize the idea that
the only serious question is suicide. Fitzgerald sensed
that. In admitting to the concept that life is absurd he
confronted the one idea totally alien to American life.

Therein lies the to-be or the not-to-be, the question of
suicide. He goes on to tell us, in a further installment,
why he had lost the ability to function. He had become
identified with the objects of his horror and his compas-
sion. He was in the shadow of the hallucinative world

that destroyed Van Gogh. He points out that when Wordsworth came to the conclusion that "there had passed away a glory from the earth," he was not compelled to pass away with it, nor did Keats, dying of consumption, ever give up his dream of being among the great poets.

Fitzgerald had been able, for many years, to hold certain opposing ideas in his mind, but when he had lost the ability to *function* he had cracked up. The myth of Sisyphus became his personal myth. While he had the resources, he was able to function in spite of the futility of the situation, but when he had overdrawn these resources, he cracked up. He lay at the bottom of the incline, the rock on top of him.

Some time before World War II made it fashionable, Fitzgerald had discovered the philosophy of the absurd. Different from the philosophers themselves, he lived and died of it. He had come, alone and prematurely, on a fact that was not yet fashionable: he had come on the experience rather than the cliché. The absurd, for Fitzgerald, was truly absurd, though nothing is ever *truly* absurd if enough clever people seem to believe in it.

The Crack-up is a report from the limbo of the All-American mind. At the point where these two opposing dreams cross, the dreamer cracks up. Such crack-ups are now common, the Nervous Breakdown now joins the All-American in a fraternity that goes deeper than his gold lodge pin. But only Fitzgerald, twenty years ago, was both sufficiently aware and sufficiently honest to look through this crack into the limbo of the mind and report what he saw.

Those deformed souls in Dante's hell, the Diviners, each so strangely twisted between the chin and the chest that they had to come backward, since seeing forward was denied them, symbolize the schizoid state of the American mind. In this confusion of dreams it is the orgiastic future that engages our daytime talents and energy, but the dark fields of the past is where we take refuge at night. The genius and progressive drive of a culture that is both the reproach and the marvel of the world is crossed with a prevailing tendency to withdraw from the world and retire into the past.

The ability of most Americans to *function*—as artists, citizens, or men of business—resides in their capacity to indulge in one of these conflicting dreams at a time; to be all for the future, that is, or all for the past. Sometimes the rhythm is that of an alternating current, the past and the present playing musical chairs, but when they meet in the mind at the same moment, that mind is apt to lose its ability to function. It cracks up.

No more curious or revealing statement than *The Crack-up* exists in our literature. After such knowledge Rimbaud wrote *A Season in Hell*, then stopped writing, and Dostoevski gave us his *Notes from Underground*.

The author of *Gatsby*, reduced to "clowning it" in the pages of *Esquire*, had to strike a "tone" that would permit him to commit hara-kiri in public. It is this tone, plus the setting of *Esquire*, that gave the statement its curious reputation. The sober-minded need not take it "seriously." What Fitzgerald *knew* can be discounted because of *where* and *how* he said it. Most readers found, as Fitzgerald had predicted, such self-revelation contemptible, and dismissed the testimony of *The Crack-up* as an ill-bred example of self-pity. It is the *giving up*, rather than the cracking up, that we find inadmissible.

The author of *The Great Gatsby*, stripped of his luck and his illusions, neither had the guts to keep it to himself nor the talent to forge new ones. In this complaint there is some justice. It is an indictment, however indirect, of the limbo of Nostalgia. But where others merely lost themselves, Fitzgerald knew where he was lost. He knew what they did not know—that from this maze there was no way out. It was neither fatigue nor the aimless wandering, but the paralysis of will that grew out of the knowledge that the past was dead, and that the present had no future. The Good, that is, in the last analysis, might not prevail. It led him to a conclusion not unlike that reached by Twain in *What is Man?*

So what? This is what I think now: that the natural state of the sentient adult is a qualified unhappiness.

Does it seem a tame monster—after the sense of horror
—to be frightened by? Qualified unhappiness, if we
examine it, is the opposite of *un*qualified happiness. It is
the opposite, that is, of Jay Gatsby, of the Goethe-Byron-
Shaw medley of Fitzgerald, of J. P. Morgan and Beau-
clerk, and St. Francis of Assisi, of all those giants who
were now relegated, as Fitzgerald tells us, to the junk
heap—the same junk heap where we will find the shoulder pads worn for one day on Princeton football field,
and that overseas cap never worn overseas.

It seems a little hard to believe—hard in the sense
that we would rather not believe it—but Master Hemingway, whose nostalgia is carefully de-mothed before he
wears it, bears witness to those things in *Death in the
Afternoon.* Speaking of the Good Old Days, those times
when men were men and bulls were tremendous, he sums
up the past, the mythic past, in these words:

Things change very much and instead of great athletes only
children play on the high-school teams now . . . they are all
children without honor, skill or virtue, much the same as these
children who now play football, a feeble game it has become,
on the high-school team and nothing like the great, mature,
sophisticated athletes in canvas elbowed jerseys, smelling vinegary
from sweated shoulder pads, carrying leather head guards, their
moleskins clotted with mud, that walked on leather-cleated shoes
that printed in the earth along beside the sidewalk in the. dusk,
a long time ago.

The irony of this passage neutralizes the charge of sentiment that it carries. Hemingway mocks it: Fitzgerald admits to its crippling effects. It seems manly to mock; it seems unmanly to acknowledge the effects. Sure, we felt that way long ago, but certainly we are not suffering from it *now*. It is this knowledge, knowledge that we *are* suffering, that deprives Fitzgerald, in spite of his power, of the manly persuasion the reader derives from Hemingway. It is classically summarized in Fitzgerald's observation that "the rich are different from us," and Hemingway's characteristic rejoinder, "Sure, they've got more money."

That kind of answer, that kind of simplification, understandably pleases the athlete in each of us, grown old, who feels that he has put such childish things behind him, and is not dying of them. Fitzgerald knew otherwise. Not only Tom Buchanan, but every American, in his fashion, went through life with invisible goal posts on his shoulders, torn from the green sod on an afternoon of never-to-be-forgotten triumph.

But was this unqualified happiness? It takes some doing; it takes the total recall of what the *ambiance* of such a dream is like, one wherein the towers of Princeton, the Triangle Club, the football shoulder pads, and the overseas cap are all transmuted by the dreamer into pure gold. On the night the world changed, Fitzgerald tells us, he hunted down the specter of womanhood and put the final touch to the adolescent season in hell. On just the other side, a mere year or two later, was paradise.

It was not the vein that played out in Fitzgerald—since nostalgia is inexhaustible—but when he knew *where* he was, when he grasped the situation, he stopped mining it. In this sense, as in many others, he reminds us of James. As a man he continued to indulge in it, but as an artist he knew it was finished. He did not know, however, that art can sometimes begin where life stops. He was too profoundly and incurably committed to life itself.

"I have now at last become a writer only," he said, but he had been suckled too long on the sweet pap of life, and the incomparable milk of wonder, to be more than a writer in name only, resigned to that fact.

. . . just as the laughing stoicism which has enabled the American negro to endure the intolerable conditions of his existence—so in my case there is a price to pay. I do not any longer like the postman, nor the grocer, nor the editor, nor the cousin's husband, and he in turn will come to dislike me, so that life will never be very pleasant again, and the sign *Cave Canem* is hung permanently just above my door.

Knowing better as an artist could not salvage him as a man. The depths of nostalgia, the slough of its despair, offered him no key to the facts of the absurd. They merely became absurd in their turn, like everything else. Having drawn on the resources he no longer possessed, and having mortgaged his remains, body and soul, he did what his countrymen now do by the thousands—he cracked up. He was different in the sense that he knew what had happened—and owned up to it.

Both *The Great Gatsby* and *Tender Is the Night* are full of personal revelation and prophecy. It is why they have such haunting immediacy when read today. The issues are still alive in anyone who is still alive. The cost of consciousness, like the expense of greatness, sometimes defies accounting, but we can see it more clearly in the life of Fitzgerald than in his works. In the life it *showed*. He was not a subtle craftsman on that plane. He was one of the lost, the truly lost; his flight established the classic itinerary, including that final ironic genuflection on the bright tan prayer rug of the Riviera.

If we reflect that Fitzgerald, while writing *Gatsby*, might have been one of the playboys in *The Sun Also Rises*—one of them, not merely with them, observing— his achievement is almost miraculous. The special charm of *Gatsby*, its durable charm, is that of recollection in tranquillity. The enchantment itself seems to come from the distance the narrator stands from the experience. The book has a serene, almost elegiac air; there is nothing frenetic or feverish about it, and the fires of spring, no longer burning, have filled the air with the scent of leaf smoke. The dark fields of the republic are bathed in a moonlit, nostalgic haze.

Fitzgerald was not yet thirty, but he was aware how well he had written. But the *meaning* of the book, its haunting tonal range, opening out into the past and portending the future, went considerably beyond both intentions and performance, into prophecy. This lucid moment of balance, when he was both fully engaged with living, yet aesthetically detached, may account for the higher level of performance than he achieved in *Tender Is the Night*. The later book is wiser, consciously wiser; the sun that had been rising is now setting, and Dick Diver is plainly stigmatized with the author's sense of his own predicament. But both books, however different in conception, close in such a manner that they blend together. The final scenes have a fugue-like harmony—an invocation in the one, a requiem in the other, to the brooding fertile god of nostalgia, dearer than life *in* life, and, at the moment of parting, sweeter than death.

Where else, we might ask, in the literature of the world has the landscape of nostalgia, created by the author, served as the refuge for both the author and his characters? Dick Diver, having had his enchantment, having listened to the dream that pandered in whispers, and having been compelled to an aesthetic contemplation he has finally come to understand, returns to the dream of West Egg, knowing the green light will be missing from Daisy's dock, knowing that the future now stands behind him, with its tail in its mouth.

So he drifts from Buffalo to Batavia, from Geneva, New York, to Hornell, where that dream of a girl, Nicole, finally lost track of him. But Fitzgerald was too honest, now, to kill him off, or to let him die. He also knew too much to let the reader see him alive. So he deposited him in that limbo where there is neither a past nor a future, the world of nostalgia where he was an aimless drifter himself. Up ahead, but not too far ahead now, faint but persistent as the music from Gatsby's parties, the blinking marsh lights of *The Crack-up* were all that shimmered in the dark fields of the republic.

My own happiness in the past often approached such an ecstacy that I could not share it even with the person dearest to me but had to walk it away in the quiet streets and lanes with only fragments of it to distill into little lines in books. . . .

What sort of happiness was this? *Un*qualified happiness, of course. The kind Gatsby had the moment he kissed Daisy, seeing, at the same moment, out of the corner of his eye that the blocks in the sidewalk seemed to form a ladder to the stars. At that moment the incomparable milk of wonder overflowed his cup of happiness, and Fitzgerald was able to distill it into more than a few little lines. In *Gatsby* this gift of hope is made flesh, and the promise is still one that Americans live by.

But the quiet streets and lanes of nostalgia soon turn upon themselves, a labyrinth without an exit, both a pub-

lic madness and a private ecstacy. The strings of reminiscence tangle on themselves, they spin a choking web
around the hero, and he must either surrender himself,
without a struggle, or risk cracking up. Fitzgerald ran
the risk. He did not, with Wolfe's adolescent bellow, try
to empty the house of its ghosts by shouting, nor did he,
like Faulkner, generate his escape with an impotent rage.
He simply faced it. But he faced it too late. Having dispensed with his resources, he cracked up. The artist in
him, as self-aware as Henry James, went on plying its
hand, sharpening all the old pencils, but the man within
him had died of nostalgia. The sign of *Cave Canem* that
hung above his door meant exactly what it said.

TWELVE

THE FUNCTION OF RAGE

WILLIAM FAULKNER

> Second, the conscious impotence of rage
> At human folly, and the laceration
> Of laughter at what ceases to amuse.
> —T. S. Eliot, "Little Gidding"

Art is not concerned with environment either. If you mean the best job ever offered to me was to become a landlord in a brothel. In my opinion it's the perfect milieu for the artist to work in. It gives him an economic freedom: he's free of fear and hunger: he has a roof over his head and nothing whatever to do except keep a few simple accounts and go once a month and pay off the local police. The place is quiet during the morning hours, which is the best time of the day for the book. There's enough social life in the evening if he wishes to participate. . . . My own experience has been that the only tools I need for my trade are paper, tobacco, food and a little whiskey.

In a widely circulated interview, William Faulkner made this statement. It is a parody, in terms of clichés, of Mr. Faulkner's romantic agony, and a pitiless example of the impotence of his rage. In this fantasy the flight is shrouded in Yellow Book *décor*: the island of peace that once lay in the territory ahead, in the dark fields of the republic, is now at the very heart of the urban corruption, the police-sanctioned whore house. Through this door the artist escapes from Aunt Sally into the world of art.

The sober reader might ask if anyone, including Faulkner, took such a statement seriously. We have the answer—which is more to our purpose than the statement—in an editorial in the *Saturday Review*. Under the heading "William Faulkner vs. the Literary Conference," the writer quotes with approval the above statement, among others, finds it comprehensive, lucid, dramatic, and honest, "in itself a work of art which should prick the conscience of ephemeral writers, yearning at any cost to find their names in print."

Here we have our old friend the raw-material myth, the home-grown, hillbilly version of Omar Khayyam, with his loaf of bread, his likker, and his nice quiet life in a house of ill fame. Implicit in this conception is the suspicion of a man who fears to be taken in by bourgeois standards, or, even worse, to be possibly mistaken for an idle intellectual, an *egghead*. If it's manly advice, and not just highfalutin talk, that our young and old writers stand in such need of, from what better podium could it be issued than the door to the brothel, under the beckoning red light?

The reader who is familiar with modern art, in particular that aspect of it we call expressionistic, may sometimes feel, as he comes to grips with Faulkner, that he has entered such scenes before, that he has, in a curiously haunting way, already experienced much of what he is reading. He will be, on occasion, troubled by a sense of *déjà vu*. The hallucinative world of Frenchman's Bend, strange as it appears, may be disturbingly familiar. It is the commonplace world of such "expressionist" artists as Chaim Soutine.

Soutine was born in Lithuania, spent most of his life as an artist in France, and there is reason to believe he had never seen a man lynched. But it is known that he once tried to hang himself. He failed in that attempt, but in one of his paintings he shows a cock that has been strung up by the neck, *plucked*. That is a commonplace sight, but as painted by Soutine we are not in the presence of a commonplace fact. What we see, and what we feel, is a life that has been strung up, stripped down, and *lynched*. Using this helpless bird the artist managed to express his sense of impotent outrage, in much the same way that a mob, using the body of a man, releases its charge of rage and violence. In one of his letters Keats describes how a street brawl that he had observed was a vulgar sight, but that the forces released in the brawl were beautiful. Such a statement might serve as a luminous definition of expressionism—a last extremity of beauty; in the noose of despair, a cry of pain that beauty makes bearable.

Soutine is a member of that branch of painting which includes Munch, Kokoschka, and Rouault, but perhaps its most celebrated figure is Van Gogh. We call them expressionists. The expression is everything. The color shrieks, the light flares and burns, faces are red, green, purple, or yellow, and objects often have the appearance of having been contorted by powerful hands. The *shaping* seems to take place before our eyes. It represents an element in what the artist is trying to express. The artist himself is possessed, we sometimes feel, by an inarticulate demon—the figure of Wolfe, with his volcanic flow of words, and his sense of self-torment, comes to mind. The expressionist and the romantic agonist have a good deal in common, and exhibit the same symptoms. What they have to say will not wait, nor lend itself to certain disciplines. They have to get it down, so to speak, while the iron is hot. Sometimes this heat is incandescent—as it is in Van Gogh, Soutine, and much of Faulkner—and sometimes, as in the rhetoric of Wolfe, it is just heat. It gives off smoke and the sound of battle, but no transforming light.

Faulkner's high regard for Wolfe, which I quoted earlier, reflects a kinship, which is apparent on the surface, as well as the torment and sense of crisis in the mind of the South. A sense of impotence drives both men to similar extremities of expression. The times are out of joint; one can do nothing, no, *nothing,* to set them right.

He spoke of the faint and ominous trembling of the guns across the hot brooding silence of the countryside, and how silence, wonder, and unspoken questions filled the hearts of all the people. . . . He spoke of the years that followed on the war when he was a stonecutter's apprentice in Baltimore, and he spoke of ancient joys and labors, forgotten acts and histories, and he spoke then with familiar memory of lost Americans—the strange lost time-far, dead Americans, the remote, voiceless and bewhiskered faces of the great Americans, who were more lost to me than Egypt, more far from me than the Tartarian coasts, more haunting strange than Cipango or the lost faces of the first dynastic kings that built the Pyramids. . . .

Who is this speaking? If we remove a few commas, if we take in the belt of sentiment a notch, it might be Faulkner. The time is the same, a lost, *lost* time, that is. Wolfe's invocation is always on the brink of tumbling into self-parody, as he grasps for Tartars, dynastic kings, and Pyramids. Faulkner's rhetoric is self-aware and all of the rhetorical strings are taut. They do not grow slack with his own emotion as he plays on them. But the music itself and its effect on the listener are similar. Time *was* when things were better. But *that* time is a *lost* time. Since one cannot bring it back, the music spins a tale of impotent rage.

If Faulkner's craft succeeds where Wolfe's fails it is perhaps less a matter of his superior talent and more a matter of their respective handicaps—rage and appetite. Appetite spread Wolfe all over the map; it dispersed both energy and talent. Rage—such a rage as Faulkner's—generates the high voltage of his art, but this rage does not free him from the delusions of nostalgia. It is the very impotence of the rage that determines the style. His medium is rhetoric, handled with such power that language spreads on the canvas like paint. In his hands it is a way of painting with words.

From a little after two oclock until almost sundown of the long still hot weary dead September afternoon they sat in what Miss Coldfield called the office because her father had called it that—a dim hot airless room with the blinds all closed and fastened for forty-three summers because when she was a girl someone had believed that light and moving air carried heat and that dark air was cooler, and which (as the sun shone fuller on that side of the house) became latticed with yellow slashes full of dust motes which Quentin thought of as being flecks of the dead old dried paint itself blown inward from the scaling blinds as the wind might have blown them.

The color in this passage is laid on thick—hot color, most of it, slashed with yellow light, the pigments blended directly on the canvas—with Miss Coldfield, dim in that dark airless room, adding the *cool* note, visually and verbally, to the picture of heat, dust, and time-tired light.

With these single, separate panels the reader can come to terms—they are windows that open both inward and outward—but when the panels multiply, when the scenes accumulate layer upon layer, like the words in the description, the mind and eye fatigue, they literally grope for air, for a door that opens onto a scene both relaxed and coherent, where the objects cease their verbal dance. But in *Absalom, Absalom!* this does not occur. We are in a gallery of mirrors that reflect only the walls covered with such paintings. The total effect is that of a mural tirelessly enlarged by a painter of genius—who does not know when to stop. But we never doubt that the artist is engaged in expressing something. Of that we are as sure as we are uncertain as to what is *expressed*.

The demon of rage, on occasion, runs as far afield, and as fruitlessly, as the baying pack of hounds that speaks for the demons of appetite. One attempts to devour, and one attempts to protest, too much. The flow of rage, like the flow of saliva, will not stop. And yet in such tales as "The Bear," and such novels as *The Sound and the Fury*, the technique is so flawless that the effect is incandescent. Craft and raw material are in such lucid balance that it seems the craftsman himself is missing. We are *within* the picture; it seems no outside force had a hand in it. Such moments, understandably, are rare, but it is thanks to such moments that we have standards of judgment. In falling below them, Faulkner passes judgment on himself. He is his own most pitiless executioner.

His finest moments are so blended of love *and* rage—his love for the past, and his outrage at the present—that this pattern of light and dark keeps his tone at a pitch. It is here, often explicitly, that his impotent and static rage, as he troubles to tell us, appears in one corner of the scene itself, like a signature. The very legs of Miss Coldfield, for example, sitting there bolt upright in the straight, hard chair, "hung . . . as if she had iron shinbones and ankles, clear of the floor with that air of impotent and static rage like children's feet. . . ."

What strikes the reader in this half-mad scene is less the madness than the *method* in it. Those legs of Miss Coldfield do not reach the floor for reasons that are both visual and crafty. Hanging like that, in suspension like that, they carry the charge of Faulkner's rage. They carry it precisely because they make no contact that would give it release. It is an example, one of many, where Faulkner's talent borders on the uncanny—the object and the charge it bears are indistinguishable. It is at such moments that Faulkner gives expression to the sense of frustration, the impotent rage that has become a daily part of the business of living, and dying, of all men of crippled good will. The man who begins that letter to the *Times*, the man who must be heard, the man who corrects an injustice, all these men find their expression in the legs of Miss Coldfield, suspended above the floor.

Expressionists are violent. It is violence that makes them expressionists. One of Edvard Munch's most powerful paintings is entitled simply "The Cry": it is a landscape that dissolves into one piercing human wail. The expressionist artist, more than any other, is the safety valve on the human boiler. It is through him that the pent-up charges find their release. It is through Faulkner that the mind of the South, time-haunted and wisteria-scented, finds such expression as is compatible with the long-dead object of its frustration. The past is dead, but long live the impotent rage.

Faulkner's most celebrated ingredient, *sex*, is a perfect medium for the discharge of emotions that are always on the brink of violence. The sense of incipient accouchement —in Faulkner's words—that seems to bathe the ripe figure of Eula Varner, hovers like an aphrodisiac mist over the somber Faulkner landscape. Like that train of swains in her wake, the reader is made aware of a "leashed turmoil of lust like so many lowering dogs after a scarce fledged and apparently unawares bitch."

This leashed and unleashed turmoil of lust is not an erotic note that Faulkner occasionally strikes. It is the atmosphere itself, the pollen-laden *ambiance* in which crime wanders in search of punishment. But this note never descends to pornography. When most explicit,

Faulkner's sex is laced with a Rabelaisian gusto and humor, a note of proportion that keeps the scene, and the subject, under firm control. The absence of erotica—the absence of the note that is sounded, time and again, in Joyce—is due less to Faulkner's craft, or his turmoil of lust, than to the fact that this lust is an impersonal passion. The characters who fall under its spell display the nature of forces, rather than personalities, and forces are not pornographic—only people are. Sex is a form of seizure, and this knowledge of sex is not merely congenial to Faulkner's rage, but makes possible scene after scene that the Greeks would have followed better than we do. We have our modern eyes on the person; Faulkner has his on the force. Few Greeks would feel estranged from a world where impotence and frustration took such a toll, and the gods, the *dead* gods, by outraged recapitulation could be evoked.

Within this violent landscape, however, like mounds of earth thrown up, then bypassed, by a flood, there are islands, remote and serene, with a mythical pastoral calm. The reader, like a man who clings to the side of a boat, sees these islands rise before him, like a mirage, right there before his eyes but forever out of his reach. It is, of course, the flood that sweeps him along that gives force and beauty to the mirage, holding the reader in the grip of an intolerable present while it woos him with a dream of the past.

The figure of Lena Grove, in *Light in August,* monumentally serene in this violent landscape, is a force that no disaster, natural or unnatural, will wash away. She would seem to be the only convincing anchor that Faulkner would allow to drag in the present. She is the great mother, the abiding earth, the patient and enduring force of life that speaks out in him again, somewhat disembodied, in his belief in the indestructibility of man. But she is a woman as well as an abstraction, and we claim her as one of us. There would seem to be no rage, no violence in her nature; the peace within her is such that rage seems childish. A man trapped and tormented beyond endurance might evoke such a dream of life to sustain him, a symbol of the good earth to which he could anchor and not be swept away. It is the surrounding tension and the incipient violence that give Lena Grove such serenity, and *Light in August* a ballast, an emotional stability, almost unique in the works of Faulkner. Her passage through the scene is like that of a healer: she radiates a palpable aura of peace and promise, so that her journey from Alabama, "a fur piece," is not unlike that of Mary and Joseph. There is a sense of mission, one that will be accomplished come hell, floods, and high water, and in the light of her passage there is a moment of peace, however disquieting, in the landscape of rage. Until the wagon that she rides in crests the hill and they see north to Jefferson, the smoke rising, there is a Biblical serenity in Faulkner's world, and a Biblical simplicity and power in his prose.

But not for long. That note is sounded, it would seem, merely to set the stage for others. First I will show you, Faulkner seems to say, something of the peace that passeth understanding, peace we have lost, so you will know and better understand the hell that is to follow. It is a calm before the storm, a woodland hush before the first crack of thunder. The driver of the wagon points his whip and says:

"See? That's a house burning."

But Lena Grove does not seem to be listening.

"My, my," she says, "here I ain't been on the road but four weeks, and now I am in Jefferson already. My, my, a body does get around."

The peace that passeth understanding passes from the scene at that point. It does not pass from the works of Faulkner, however, but is enshrined, for safekeeping, at the heart of his mythic wilderness, at the very core of his private territory ahead. Here lies the innocent land, the flowering wilderness, where Ikkemotubbe taught the steamboat where to walk, and the white man's world of rage and violence is kept at bay; or, rather, it is laughed, with a high mythical laughter, off the face of the earth.

Faulkner's noble savages, however, are not the wooden Indians of Fenimore Cooper, trackless phantoms in hand-painted woods, but truly mythic creations, bigger than life, who serve as the shrines for his incomparable humor.

Here the frontier farce of exaggeration—the celebrated jumping frog of Mark Twain—is elevated, with no apparent sign of strain, to the level of the mythic fable. There is nothing in literature to compare with the fabulous courtship by David Hogganbeck and Ikkemotubbe of Herman Basket's sister, that primal and ever-receding vision of womanly loveliness. This marvelous tale, like a stream of clear and undefiled water, winds and unwinds its way through the Faulkner labyrinth. It remains sweet and pure, where others become corrupt and befouled. It never hurries, where others rush toward an impending flood. But it is *echt* Faulkner, a crystalline essense; the cloud of rage has blown away and nothing remains but the sound of the lovers in their timeless pursuit. It hardly seems to matter, amidst these forest murmurs, that this vision of loveliness is won by another, that this *Ewig-Weibliche* is the property of that idler Log-in-the-Creek. That, indeed, is essential to the picture; one of the scenic props of the mythic wilderness, that the ne'er-do-well, the tireless idler, sprawled on the floor with his harmonica cupped to his mouth, should vanquish the giants who clank their armor in the sun.

In this enchanted land, from which rage has been banished, we see how rich a vein of myth the writer inherits, and how deep and true it runs in the American grain. If Faulkner wants to tell us *this* place will endure he has earned the right. Here he no longer speaks for himself, or Frenchman's Bend, or even time out of mind.

Here he is the mythic voice of the green continent itself. That fresh green breast of the world that once flowered for Fitzgerald—and Dutch sailors' eyes. Here he holds his rage; he is all ears to the voice that panders in such persuasive whispers to the last and greatest of all human dreams. For a transitory moment he holds his breath in the presence of this voice, this territory ahead, compelled to a creation he hardly understood, face to face for the last time with something commensurate with his capacity for wonder.

To David Hogganbeck's statement that there is, for all men, just one wisdom, Ikkemotubbe replied: "Aihee. At least, for all men one same heartbreak."

This wisdom, indeed, has its indestructible elements. Paradise Lost, never to be regained, still generates in Adam such dreams as bear the telling, and Faulkner testifies to one that is both universal and American. To that extent, who can say that the times have changed? "One same heartbreak" is a link that joins men where others have failed. In this landscape of heartbreak Faulkner joins hands with the mournful, myth-haunted knight of Cervantes, neither the first nor the last man to take refuge in the mythic past. With Cervantes he has earned the right to remind us that although it is Sancho who inherits the world, it is the Helmet of Mambrino, that illusion, that makes it desirable.

Part Five

THE AMERICAN SCENE

THIRTEEN

OBJECTS AND PLACES

To be at all critically, or as we have been fond of calling it, analytically minded—over and beyond an inherent love of the many-colored picture of things—is to be subject to the superstition that objects and places, coherently grouped, disposed for human use and addressed to it, must have a sense of their own, a mystic meaning proper to themselves to give out: to give out, that is, to the participant at once so interested and so detached as to be moved to a report of the matter.

If we were to ask Crèvecoeur's perennial question, What is an American? the man most qualified to give us an answer is the man least likely to be asked—the exile Henry James.

James, the *dis*patriate, and Tocqueville, the tourist, divide the question between them. The latter gives us more of the outward form, while the province of James resides in the mystic meaning proper to themselves that objects and places give out. It was this meaning James wanted, and in *The American Scene* it was what he found.

It is significant, in this connection, that Tocqueville is a familiar, accepted classic, while *The American Scene* is one of the many widely unread books of James. We are at home with the outward form, and with the deductions that are drawn from such forms, but the world of James is not a simple display of pregnant artifacts. The artifacts are *there*, but the mind of James is concerned with their vibrations. He is out for bigger game than appearances. He returned to America with the explicit intention of tracking it down. The superstition that all these objects and places—this flood tide of unprocessed raw material—had not merely a meaning proper to themselves that they would surrender to some participant, but that Henry James was the proper participant he knew from the start, the only one both so interested and so detached as to be moved to a report of the matter.

On the evidence, and on nothing else, it is possible to say that no other book contains so much of the American scene, since no other book has so much to give out. The detachment that exile afforded James is different from the detachment it afforded Tocqueville, since the consciousness of James is essentially that of the scene itself. He is consciously self-conscious; the impressions he records are not those of a traveler, but those of a native who is finally aware of what it is he feels. In James, the American scene becomes articulate. No greater irony is possible than that of James, the most fully conscious mind and talent of the century, speaking for a nation primarily *non*-conscious, and proud of it. This spectacle understandably goes unappreciated, since it is almost impossible to grasp: one of the last extremities of rawness finding its voice in the last extremity of sensibility.

The highest luxury of all, the supremely expensive thing, is constituted privacy—and yet it was the supremely expensive thing that the good people supposed themselves to be getting. . . .

In such a nutshell, one of thousands, lies the kernel of such matters as we now discuss under such attractive slogans as the New Conformity or the Lonely Crowd. James does not raise his voice, he does not point, nothing stands in isolation or cries its moral, but it is all one piece of cloth, the first tailored fitting of the Gray Flannel Suit.

There were the two sexes, I think, and the range of age, but, once the one comprehensive type was embraced, no other signs of differentiation. How should there have been when the men were consistently, in all cases, thoroughly obvious products of the business-block, the business-block unmitigated by any other influence definite enough to name, and the women were, under the same strictness, the indulgent ladies of such lords. The business-block has perhaps, from the north-east to south-west, its fine diversities, but any variety so introduced eluded even the most brooding of analysts.

The year is 1905. The place is Palm Beach. But the observation is both timeless and placeless. It is still what there is to be seen in the American scene.

If we ask ourselves why the detachment of James is comparable to that of the detachment of Tocqueville, his exile, his point of view as an outsider, is only part of the answer. We have had hundreds of exiles, and many of them talented. The heart of the matter is that James is not a victim of nostalgia. Among all of these exiles, he alone is not a captive of the past. James is a free man in the sense that Tocqueville is free. Each can feel confidence in his impressions, knowing that these impressions are not hopelessly betrayed by nostalgic ties, or concealed emotional commitments. The act of will that James displayed in his *dis*patriation was an act of severance from such commitments. It is this that leaves him—as he knows and tells us—more of a participant than ever before. He returns as a native to repossess, fully, what was both unpossessed and dispossessed.

I would take my stand [he tells us] on my gathered impressions, since it was all for them, for them only, that I returned; I would, in fact, go to the stake for them. . . .

The word "impression," in this connection, will strike the American mind as strange. An impression is not something that we go to the stake for. But an impression, for James, is nothing less than the thing itself. The specific gravity of this word, for James, is at the farthest remove from that of normal usage, but is of the same value, precisely, as the impressionism of Cézanne. All that is transitory has been processed out of it. Cézanne's effort to "realize his sensations" is parallel to the effort of James—an act of possession, one for which each man would go to the stake. The year that Cézanne died at Aix, Henry James was in America, gathering impressions of the same permanence.

Freedom from nostalgia—a comparative freedom, deliberately cultivated to secure a larger bounty—isolates James, more than his exile, from the traditional assumptions of the American mind. That prevailing tendency to withdraw from everything complex, into anything simple, was a provincial and crippling tendency he early recognized. What the brave new world called for was a concept that was *bigger* than the provincials' flattering notions of the wilderness. Few things describe the isolation of James so well as the fact that in going to Europe, in going when he did, he appeared to be doing merely what was fashionable. His lonely pilgrimage was just fifty years ahead of its time. What he gathered from it, however—free of the apparatus of nostalgia and rebellion—appears to be still another fifty years ahead of us. That *figure* of James, impressively at home in the *haut monde* society of fashion, has effectively concealed the avant-garde artist, the holder of dangerous opinions, and the prophet on whom nothing was lost in *The American Scene*. In this book the virus of suggestion attacks him at every pore. The book is made almost impenetrable by impressions, and is grained with his craft. In it he comes to terms with America, and indicates, in his exhaustive fashion, what America must do to come to terms with *him*. It boils down to an old challenge. What America must do is come of age.

In failing to come to terms with James—a failure that always has so much to recommend it—the new start that Van Wyck Brooks did so much to encourage turned out, on examination, to be the same old story. In calling for the liberated native artist, Brooks was behind, rather than ahead of, James. The writers who came of age, almost without exception, were those who came to terms with old-world standards, and through their exile came to terms, each in his own fashion, with the American scene. This was what James recommended, through his example, and what he was the first, in his works, to achieve.

Nothing will better illustrate the uniqueness of James —the genius that results from a man's limitations—than "the pair of summer girls and a summer youth" that he encountered touring in New England. The phrase itself, so deliciously heightened by the repetition of the word summer, evokes the scene as skillfully as Chekhov, and establishes its tone. If we know our James we know that nothing will *happen*—or rather that it is already *happen-*

ing, and will go on happening without anything specific having occurred. This is not the way of life, of normal life, but it is the normal nature of consciousness. James knows what will happen before it happens, and the events, indeed, are matters of little interest. What matters is the scene itself, the virus of suggestion that has him vibrating, and what he gives us is a tone poem on the theme "a pair of summer girls and a summer youth." They share the open air, and the space on top of a coach with him.

That curiosity held its breath, in truth, for fear of breaking the spell—the spell of the large liberty with which a pair of summer girls and a summer youth, from the hotel, took all nature and all society (so far as society was present on the top of the coach) into the confidence of their personal relation. Their personal relation—that of the young man was with the two summer girls, whose own was all with *him*; any other, with their mother, for instance, who sat speechless and serene beside me, with the other passengers, with the coachman, the guard, the quick-eared four-in-hand, being for the time completely suspended. The freedoms of the young three—who were, by the way, not in their earliest bloom either—were thus bandied in the void of the gorgeous valley without even a consciousness of its shriller, its recording echoes. The whole phenomenon was documentary; it started for the restless analyst, innumerable questions, amidst which he felt himself sink beyond his depth. The immodesty was too colossal to be anything but innocence—yet the innocence, on the other hand, was too colossal to be anything but inane. And they were alive, the slightly stale three: they talked, they laughed, they sang, they shrieked, they romped, they scaled the pinnacle of publicity and perched on it, flapping their wings; whereby they were shown in possession of many of the movements of life. Life, however, involved some degree of experience—if only the experience, for instance, of the summer apparently just spent, at great cost, in the gorgeous valley. How was that, how was perception of any concurrent presence, how was the human or the social function at all compatible with the *degree* of the inanity?

How many summer novels—including last summer's —have explored, for thousands of pages, this same situation but found less in it? Summer lovers still scale, in a variety of ways, the pinnacle of publicity, but are not often either so closely, or so lethally, observed.

The reader raised on Hemingway, Caldwell, or Farrell, seeing only what is *absent*, not what is *present*, will conclude that the picture frankly lacks its subject—the *sexual* element. That element is lacking for an obvious reason. It is not, in this scene, the subject. What James seeks to observe he observes precisely—*a pair of summer girls and a summer youth*. On that subject he penetrates to the core, to the question of motives, to the sense of unawareness, to the singular spell of that large liberty in which they were all, there on the top of the coach, so colossally suspended. His subject is this microcosmic sample of innocent inanity. If we think how Hemingway, on the one hand, and Sinclair Lewis, perhaps, on the other, would have dealt with *this* subject, would have ignored it, that is, we can see that the impression James records gives off the more durable vibrations. This pair of summer girls, and this youth, have the anonymous air of permanence. They *represent*, they represent so many summers, girls, and youths. They are neither lost, in their innocent fatuity, nor are they played with as comical caricatures. The pinnacle on which they perch, flapping their wings, is serving the same stale purpose today.

The note of *manners*: that is the note, above all, that he wants to catch. The reader who comes freshly to James must freshen up his feeling for the word "manners." James never means good or bad. He wants to know only where and what they are, and what they have to tell. For James it is the manners, not the voices, that tell all.

That pair of summer girls and that summer youth do not make love before our eyes, or much of anything else, since they are making and revealing much more in the mind of James. What they are making does not make for drama, nor for the novels of Balzac and Tolstoi, but it makes for what the author is up to: it makes for James. The art of James, the consciousness of James, is a faculty that exists in and through such dramatic defects, not in spite of them. This does not explain away his failures, nor the ambivalence that we feel to be evasion, but the

awareness James lifts to the level of genius finds in
everything its drama. It is, in James, a state of awareness,
rather than an arrangement of events. In *The American
Scene* he put this awareness to the acid test. He proved
himself, in so doing, to be precisely what Edmund Wilson—a penetrating and sympathetic critic of James—
concluded that he was not—a prophet.

Mr. Wilson was thinking of events, in particular events
of a political nature, the lights that were about to go out
over Europe, of which James was almost deliberately
unaware. When this world fell on him, no man in England seemed less prepared. But the prophetic vein in
James runs deeper than the events it anticipates. Naïve
politically, as remote from the world, at Rye, as Hawthorne had been at Salem, James cannot tell us what
events will occur, but whether, if, and when they occur,
they matter. This, he would point out, is a matter of
consciousness. To the extent that the artist is supremely
conscious, his impressions will anticipate the future as
richly as they evoke and incorporate the past. We know
that they will, since that is precisely what *The American
Scene* does.

In stating flatly his willingness to go to the stake for
his *impressions*, James threw down a gauntlet that few
have taken the trouble to pick up. He says, in so many
words, this is *it*. The audacity of this assumption is more
than matched by the performance, but few—even few
James readers—seem to have cared. They didn't *want* his

America if they were English, and if they were American the author was an exile, and no longer fashionable. This reduced the book's circulation, but in any case it would have had few readers. In *The American Scene* James is simply too much for all of us.

Judgments of almost lethal penetration are rendered without the trace of an air of judgment.

It in any case remains vivid that American life may, as regards much of its manifestation, fall upon the earnest view as a society of women "located" in a world of men, which is so different a matter from a collection of men of the world; the men supplying, as it were, all the canvas, and the women all the embroidery.

In this impression, at the turn of the century, James not merely anticipates much of the fiction that we call modern, but renders it, by the same token, obsolete. What indeed, we must ask, would such a mind grasp if among us today? We can rest assured it would not be trafficking in its own clichés. The American novelist, mid-century, will read this book with fear and trembling, since it puts in question the very reason for his existence— his contemporaneity. Having climbed to some pinnacle, or dived to some depth, he turns to see that James, like Kilroy, was already there.

There is such a thing, in the United States, it is hence to be inferred, as freedom to grow up to be blighted, and it may be the only freedom in store for the smaller fry of future generations.

When the Man in the Gray Flannel Suit tells us all, this is what he does not tell us. After all, it would seem to be the freedom in which he takes the most pride. Before we question him on that, however, we might ask how many books, unaware of the question, testified, unknowingly, to its answer. The early power and the late ineptitude of such a writer as Dreiser lie in his awareness of such a fact but his inability to grasp its implications. He believed himself anchored in eternal truth, rather than in one of the sand pits of freedom. What we admire in Dreiser is precisely what we suspect in James. We like the nonconscious life, compassionately dwelt on, where the forces that salvage or destroy us lie beyond our power, and lend a certain pathos to our incompetence. The consciousness of James deprives us of this consolation. To the four consoling freedoms, one must be added: the appalling and visible freedom to be blighted.

A man's genius cannot be formulated, but what James brings to the American scene is his freedom, his freedom as an artist, from the prevailing clichés. The word "freedom," itself, is one of them. He did not abuse it: he was merely aware of the treacherous life that such freedom led.

But it is not only manners, and institutions, that make up the American scene. With his characteristic sense of proportion he knew that this scene was dominated by Nature. Even by a NATURE writ large, as Lawrence said. When he observes that Nature, he meets our nature writers on their home ground. The genius of James is most vividly apparent if we compare his impressions of nature with that master of nature Thoreau. Here is a passage from *Walden*, a classical passage, one that exhibits both nature and the author at their best:

This is a delicious evening, when the whole body is one sense, and imbibes delight through every pore. I go and come with a strange liberty in Nature, a part of herself. As I walk along the stony shore of the pond in my shirt sleeves, though it is cool as well as cloudy and windy, and I see nothing special to attract to me, all the elements are unusually congenial to me.

Here is James, the city-bred man, passing through a scene equally delicious:

The apples are everywhere and every interval, every old clearing, an orchard; they have "run down" from neglect and shrunken from cheapness—you pick them up from under your feet but to bite into them, for fellowship, and throw them away. . . . The question of the encircled waters too, larger and smaller—that again was perhaps an ado about trifles; but you can't, in such conditions, and especially at first, resist the appeal of their extraordinarily mild faces and wooded brims, with the various choice spots where the great straight pines, interspace behind them, and yielding to small strands as finely curved as the eyebrows of beauty, make the sacred grove and the American classic temple, the temple for the worship of the evening sky, the cult of the Indian canoe, of Fenimore Cooper, of W. C.

Bryant, of the immortalizable water-fowl. They look too much alike, the lakes and the ponds, and this is, indeed, all over the world, too much a reproach to lakes and ponds—to all save the pick of the family, say, like George and Champlain; the American idea, moreover, is too inveterately that woods shall grow thick to the water. . . . But that boat across the water is safe, is sustaining as far as it goes; it puts out from the cove of romance, from the inlet of poetry, and glides straight over, with muffled oar, to the—well, to the right place.

One is in America, in the *scene*, one is aware of the beauty of the American landscape, but in the closing phrase, with its affectionate irony, one is part of a larger landscape than the scene itself. This is criticism, sympathetic but just, an awareness that there is more to the world—however delicious the evening—than the spot that one stands on. This large sense, this more comprehensive scene, is lacking in Thoreau. He is unable, as is James, to smile with affection at his own indulgence, and recognize the nostalgic coves, and clichéd inlets, of romance. Thoreau is taken in by his own talent; James is not. That boat that puts out from the cove of romance and glides with muffled oar to the—well, the right place is a supreme instance of James's masterly interest and detachment. Here he lucidly anticipates the urban-woodland note of such a writer as E. B. White. This note, needless to say, was *not* the note being struck at the time. That kind of self-awareness, that kind of detachment, implied a certain criticism of the prevailing tendencies. The cult of the immortalized waterfowl—still with us in the *décor* of the streamlined office—owes as much, if not more, to Thoreau as to the ever-rippling waters of Minnehaha. James had an eye for the bird, but he did not swallow it, feathers and all. Not lost on him was the water dripping from the muffled oars.

Where the manners are dense, vibrating with implications, James is understandably at his best, and the manners are densest in the cities, where the men live downtown and the women live uptown; where the men are busy supplying the canvas, and the women are busy supplying the embroidery.

From the moment it is adequately borne in mind that the business man in the United States, may with no matter what dim struggles, gropings, yearnings, never hope to be anything *but* a business man, the size of the field he abdicates is measured, as well as the fact of the other care to which his abdication hands it over. It lies there waiting, pleading from all its pores, to be occupied—the lonely waste, the boundless, gaping void of "society"; which is but a name for all the other so numerous relations with the world he lives in that are imputable to a civilized being. Here it is then that the world he lives in accepts its doom and becomes, by his default, subject and plastic to his mate; his default having made, all around him, the unexampled opportunity of the woman—which she would have been an incredible fool not to pounce upon. It needs little contact with American life to see how she *has* pounced, and how, outside business, she has made it over in her image. . . .

That is the *scene*, but the restless analyst cannot resist a prophetic comment.

She has meanwhile probably her hours of amazement at the size of her windfall; she cannot quite live without wonder at the oddity of her so "sleeping" partner, the strange creature, by her side, with his values and his voids, but who is best known to her as having yielded what she would have clutched to the death.

How many books yet to be published will exploit this situation without grasping this knowledge? How many tracts, treatises, and questionnaires, how many Freudian analyses and Kinsey interviews, have used, abused, and toyed with this fact but remained aloof from this understanding? This *successful* rupture of a universal law—as James defines it elsewhere—was the one impression that overpowered all of the others.

The only thing is that, from the moment the painter begins to look at American life, brush in hand, he is in danger of seeing, in comparison, almost nothing else in it—nothing, that is, so characteristic as this apparent privation, for the man, of his right kind of woman, and this apparent privation, for the woman, of her right kind of man.

At the time this observation was made Americans, in large numbers, were reading *To Have and to Hold*, by Mrs. Johnston, *Lady Rose's Daughter*, by Mrs. Humphry Ward, along with current best sellers by Harold Bell Wright, Gene Stratton Porter, and Zane Grey. Things were pretty much the same as they are now. It was the Girl of the Golden West who beckoned to the businessman, and the Man who *was* a Man who beckoned to his wife.

James is not through, however. He goes on to say:

The right kind of woman for the American man may really be, of course, as things are turning out for him, the woman as to whom his most workable relation is to support her and bear with her—just as the right man for the American woman may really be the man who intervenes in her life only by occult, by barely divinable, by practically disavowed courses.

If we turn from the inhabitants to the scene itself, to that downtown world where the Man does his living, James takes a look at the garden where the Man in the Gray Flannel Suit will sprout.

There are new cities enough about the world, goodness knows, and there are new parts enough of old cities . . . but the newness of New York, unlike even that of Boston—I seemed to discern —had this mark of its very own, that it effects one, in every case, as having treated itself as still more provisional, if possible, than any poor dear little interest of antiquity it may have annihilated. *The very sign of its energy is that it doesn't believe in itself; it fails to succeed, even at a cost of millions, in persuading you that it does.* . . . The difficulty with the compromised charmer is just this constant inability to convince; to convince ever, I mean, that

she is serious, serious about any form whatever, or anything but
that perpetual passionate pecuniary purpose which plays with all
forms, which derides and devours them, though it may pile up
the cost of them in order to rest awhile, spent and haggard, in
the illusion of their finality. [Italics mine]

One can neither speak for nor against such a writer.
One can only quote. The resonant density of the mind of
James, the style that fills, like a liquid, every crevice of
its subject, cannot be paraphrased or poured to cool in
quotable remarks. The impression is the fissioning rays
of the subject itself.

The perception of this truth grows for you by your simply
walking up Fifth Avenue and pausing a little in presence of
certain forms, certain exorbitant structures, in other words, the
elegant domicilary, as to which the illusion of finality was within
one's memory magnificent and complete, but as to which one
feels today that their life wouldn't be, as against any whisper
of a higher interest, worth an hour's purchase. They sit there
in the florid majesty of the taste of their time—a light now, alas,
generally clouded; and I pretend of course to speak, in alluding
to them, of no individual case of danger or doom. . . . Again
and again, in the upper reaches, you pause with that pity; you
learn, on the occasion of a kindly glance up and down a quiet
street (there being objects and aspects in many of them appealing
to kindness) that such and such a house, or a row, is "coming
down"; and you gasp, in presence of the elements involved, at
the strangeness of the moral so pointed. It rings out like the crack

of that lash in the sky, the play of some mighty teamster's whip.
. . . "No"—this is the tune to which the whip seems flourished—
"there's no step at which you shall rest, no form, as I'm constantly showing you, to which, consistently with my interests,
you *can*. I build you up but to tear you down, for if I were to
let sentiment and sincerity once take root, were to let any tender-
ness of association once accumulate, or any 'love of the old'
once pass unsnubbed, what would become of *us*, who have our
hands on the whipstock, please?"

As if determined to test his impressions, James exposed
himself to such ornaments as Newport, Salem, and Con-
cord, to Charleston as well as Washington and Rich-
mond, but more instructive is a visit he made to that
"terrible little Ellis island," that welcome mat to the
cavernously hospitable American house.

I think indeed that the simplest account of the action of Ellis
island on the spirit of any sensitive citizen who may have happened to "look in" is that he comes back from this visit not at
all the same person that he went. He has eaten of the tree of
knowledge, and the taste will forever be in his mouth. He had
thought he knew before, thought he had the sense of the degree
in which it is his American fate to share the sanctity of his American consciousness, the intimacy of his American patriotism, with
the inconceivably alien: but the truth had never come to him
with such force. In the lurid light projected on it by those courts
of dismay it shakes him—or I like at least to imagine it shakes
him—to the depths of his being; I like to think of him, I posi-

tively *have* to think of him as going about ever afterwards with a new look, for those who can see it, in his face, the outward sign of a new chill in his heart. So is, stamped for detection, the unquestionably privileged person who has had an apparition, seen a ghost in his supposedly safe house. Let not the unwary, therefore, visit Ellis island.

We are accustomed to that chill in the heart today, the courts of dismay being a modern institution, but here again James, his finger on the pulse, looks the seemingly robust patient in the eye and wonders how much of the truth he can charitably share with his family. The answer is, not much. What is alien to us should understandably remain unmentioned and inconceivable.

Even as he tells us that New York was now too huge a spectacle for any single reflector, too monstrous a phenomenon for any future Zola, the shape of things to come rises, like a genie, from his observations.

That conviction came to me most perhaps while I gazed across at the special skyscraper that overhangs poor old Trinity to the north—a south face as high and wide as the mountain wall that drops the Alpine avalanche, from time to time, on the village, and the village spire, at its foot; the interest of this case being above all, as I learned, to my stupefaction, in the fact that the very creators of the extinguisher are the church wardens themselves, or at least the trustees of the church property. What was the case but magnificent for pitiless ferocity?—that inexorable law of the growing invisibility of churches, their everywhere reduced or abolished presence, which is nine-tenths of their virtue, receiving thus, at such hands, its supreme consecration.

What, indeed, is the case but magnificent for pitiless ferocity? The trustee and the church warden, now interchangeable roles, still pay their Christian tribute in those quaint little places their money, their energy, and such powers as they possess have so pitifully dwarfed. Henry Adams, too, observed this displacement of the Virgin and the Dynamo; the law, in each case, pitiless in its ferocity.

The triumph of James's sensibility, what the Master could do with the virus of suggestion, is in the rendezvous of James with the lobby of the Waldorf-Astoria. This experience fairly carries him away, and is perhaps his richest lode of prophecy. When we reflect that the lobby, the hotel lobby, has become a scenic prop in American life and fiction, it is a characteristic instance of James's awareness of what, in that sense, *bristles* with a maximum intensity.

The moral in question, the high interest of the tale, is that you are in presence of a revelation of the possibilities of the hotel —for which the American spirit has found so unprecedented a use and a value; leading it on to express so a social, indeed positively an esthetic ideal, and making it so, at this supreme pitch, a synonym for civilization, for the capture of conceived manners themselves, that one is verily tempted to ask if the hotel spirit may not just *be* the American spirit most seeking and most finding itself. . . . It is an expression of the gregarious state break-

ing down every barrier but two—one of which, the barrier
consisting of the high pecuniary tax, is the immediately obvious.
The other, the rather more subtle, is the condition, for any
member of the flock, that he or she—in other words especially
she—be presumably "respectable," be, that is, not discoverably
anything else. The rigour with which any appearance of pursued
or desired adventure is kept down—adventure in the florid sense
of the word, the sense in which it remains a euphemism—is not
the least interesting note of the whole immense promiscuity. Pro-
tected at those two points the promiscuity carries, through the
rest of the range, everything before it.

In this instance the analysis is the curtain that rises on
the scene.

It sat there, it walked and talked, and ate and drank, and
listened and danced to music, and otherwise revelled and roamed,
and bought and sold, and came and went there, all on its own
splendid terms and with an encompassing material splendor a
wealth and variety of constituted picture and background, that
might well feed it with the finest illusions about itself. It paraded
through halls and saloons in which art and history, in masquerad-
ing dress, muffled almost to suffocation as in the gold brocade of
their pretended majesties and their conciliatory graces, stood
smirking in its passage with the last cynicism of hypocrisy. The
exhibition is wonderful for that, for the suggested sense of
promiscuity which manages to be at the same time an inordinate
untempered monotony . . . and I confess that all gave way, in
my mind, to a single irresistible obsession. This was just the ache
of envy of the spirit of a society which had found there, in its

prodigious public setting, so exactly what it wanted. One was in presence, as never before, of a realized ideal of that childlike rush and surrender to it and clutch at it which one was so repeatedly to recognize, in America, as the note of the supremely gregarious state. It made the whole vision unforgettable, and I am now carried back to it, I confess, in musing hours, as to one of my few glimpses of perfect human felicity.

For its breadth and lucidity, its lyrical flow of perception, for its orphic grasp of the meaning at work in what has meaning, I doubt that this passage has its equal in literature. Here, as throughout this incandescent book, James is simply too much for us. There is one classical deploy to be taken in defense, and for more than fifty years we have resorted to it. Our head dipped into the sand, we simply pretend that James is not there. His exile, combined with our indifference, spares us the necessity of coming to terms with either his genius or this prophetic portrait of ourselves.

It is usually ignored, or forgotten, that if the love of art and culture took James to France, the stifling conventions of art so necessary to the French ego led him to go to England, where the winds of opinion had freer play. It was always more life that James wanted, rather than less. Narrowness, native or imported, acted as a damper on his consciousness. It was this sense of suffocation, of the mind in wraps, that troubled him most about the American scene. When the scene itself seemed to speak to him, saying, "See what I'm making of all this—see what I'm making!" James, in exasperation, replied:

I see what you are *not* making, oh, what you are so vividly not; and how can I help it if I am subject to that lucidity?—which appears never so welcome to you, for its measure of truth, as it ought to be. . . . If I were one of the painted savages you have dispossessed, or even some tough reactionary trying to emulate him, what you are making would doubtless impress me more than what you are leaving unmade; for in that case it wouldn't be to *you* I should be looking in any degree for beauty or charm. Beauty or charm would be for me in the solitude you have ravaged, and I should owe you my drudge for every disfigurement and every violence, for every wound with which you have caused the face of the land to bleed. No, since I accept your ravage, what strikes me is the long list of the arrears of your undone; and so constantly, right and left, that your pretended message of civilization is but a colossal recipe for the creation of arrears, and of such as can but remain forever out of hand. You touch the great lonely land—as one feels it still to be—only to plant upon it some ugliness about which, never dreaming of the graces or apology of contrition, you then proceed to brag with a cynicism all your own. You convert the large and noble sanities that I see around me, you convert them one after the other to crudities, to invalidities, hideous and unashamed; and you so leave them to add to the number of myriad aspects you simply spoil, of the myriad unanswerable questions that you scatter about as some monstrous unnatural mother might leave a family of unfathered infants on doorsteps or waiting rooms.

Such is the gist of his indictment. It is rendered with more than a perceptible tremor in his voice. Whether we are or are not "a colossal recipe for the creation of arrears," it is the judgment of a man who has been moved to report on the matter out of his love, his concern, and his intuitive grasp of the mystic meaning proper to itself that this scene gives out. It is a judgment sensitive to, but not crippled by, nostalgia. *No*—he tells us—*since I accept your ravage,* what strikes me is the long list of the arrears. It is the present, not the past, that generates his rage. James does not want things as they were, he asks only that the process of becoming should finally become something of value, not just one more thing to tear down, in order to put something else up.

This is not the complaint of the nature lover, bewailing the loss of a bird sanctuary, but the concern of a man who sees a principle of waste that feeds on itself. But in coming to terms with this indictment—insofar as we believe it to be accurate—we may be led to conclusions James did not anticipate: conclusions of our own. The recipe for arrears, which we still see all around us, may have a concealed from James what it revealed to Tocqueville. James's sense of the past—the converse of nostalgia—his sympathy for all things disposed for human use and addressed to it, made it impossible for him to come to terms with the force, the monster, that ravaged everything in sight. And yet it is such a monster, such a waste-breeding dragon, that symbolizes the Spirit of the Place. His motto might be *Let Nothing Stand,* since all things stand in the way of Progress. Traditions and customs, great and small buildings, and, in our time, great and small reputations are thrown into the hopper and ground up, so that fresh reputations can take their places. We have, indeed, reached such a pass that the new is obsolete on its appearance; early obsolescence is a built-in characteristic of a wide range of products. Automobiles, appliances, Hollywood starlets, and lending-library fiction are all produced on the principle of the quick turnover. That they will soon be displaced is the reason for their existence. Time Marches On.

We have not merely reached such a pass, but we have come to recognize it as the *system.* But how *new* is it? James was perhaps the first to see the breadth, the human breadth, of its application, but it is here that Tocqueville might have cautioned him. As profoundly as James had grasped the system, was he not looking at the scene for irrelevant matter? Beauty and charm—was there reason to suppose this was what Americans were up to? Not for long. Ten years before Henry James was born, that restless analyst Tocqueville, browsing and probing on the water front, came up with this impression:

I accost an American sailor, and inquire why the ships of his country are built so as to last but for a short time; he answers without hesitation, that the art of navigation is everyday making such progress, that the finest vessel would become almost useless if it lasted beyond a few years. In these words, which fell accidentally, and on a particular subject, from an uninstructed man, I recognize *the general and systematic idea upon which a great people direct all their concerns.*

Aristocratic nations are naturally too apt to narrow the scope of human perfectibility; democratic nations, to expand it beyond reason. [Italic mine]

Little new has been said about America since *The American Scene.* The lonely crowd, the perpetual pecuniary passion, the uptown world of women, the downtown world of men—"what was the case," for the restless analyst, "but magnificent for pitiless ferocity"? No appraisal can be more persuasive nor indictment more lethal, since it flows from a generous nature, and a disinterested mind. Our pretended message for civilization is more than ever a "recipe for the creations of arrears," and our freedom is increasingly a freedom to be blighted. As the books of self-praise roll off our presses, extolling our glorious past, and evoking our fabulous future, the *present* testifies to the appalling accuracy of James's perceptions—the very hallmark of its energy being that it does not believe in itself. The impressions on which James would make his stand have in this half-century found their confirmation. We now live in a world that he grasped better than we grasp it ourselves.

It was James's distinction in *The American Scene* to have been the first to view that scene from the *present,* free from visions of the future and crippling commitments to the past. It is this *presentness* that resulted in impressions consistently prophetic. In this light it is important to remember that this book of impressions was left unfinished; it tapers off, it dies off like a voice, rather than ends. A man whose very genius was parenthesis knew that here, above all, was a subject, for him of all subjects, one on which he would never say the last word.

Part Six

THE TERRITORY AHEAD

FOURTEEN

THE IMMEDIATE PRESENT

If I have emphasized technique, the primacy of technique, over such things as experience and raw material, it is because the primacy of life—in the American scene—is obvious. Such balance as needs redressing is all one way. The problem of tradition and the individual talent might be expressed in this manner: Until the life of literature is equal in importance to the personal life of the writer, his personal life will seldom enter the stream of literature. It is in the interests of such life—the life in literature—that technique is indispensable. Had Proust not *lived* a life, and in his own fashion, his cork-lined chamber would have been merely his coffin, not the crucible where he transmuted what life he had lived into art. What the artist seems to distill from the air is the shape in which the material is forged. But there is no substitute for the material itself—the *life* in literature.

If the modern temper, as distinct from the romantic, lies in the admission that men are mortal, this admission determines the nature of the raw material with which the artist must work. An element of despair, a destructive element, is one of the signs by which we shall know him; the other is the constructive use to which this element is put. It distinguishes this artist from the seriously hopeful, or the hopefully serious, who cannot bring themselves to admit of the contemporary facts. These men *know* better, almost without exception, but their hope lies in the refusal to admit what they know. This common failure of admission characterizes their work and blights their hope. The modern temper finds its facts, and its hope, in the statement by Albert Camus: "I want to know if I can live with what I know and only with that." Nothing could be farther from the Bohemian traditions, the irresponsible clichés of the artist's life, than this discipline of facts he must face and master in the name of his art. He must become that paradox, both a visionary and a realist. These are strange gods to reconcile in one man, and in one art. To what extent does the modern artist succeed, to what extent does he fail? We need representative men, and we have them, in James Joyce, T. S. Eliot, and D. H. Lawrence, all men, in their fashion, after strange gods.

In Joyce's *Portrait of the Artist as a Young Man,* the young man, Stephen Dedalus, makes this confession to his friend Cranly:

You made me confess the fears that I have. But I will tell you also what I do not fear. I do not fear to be alone or to be spurned for another or to leave whatever I have to leave. And I am not afraid to make a mistake, even a great mistake, a lifelong mistake and perhaps as long as eternity too.

In this statement we have the temperament, the devotion, and the prophetic life of the artist. We also have more than a hint that he is after strange gods. He does not fear to make a mistake: a lasting mistake. We know, now, to what extent Joyce realized this prophecy, although we cannot judge, as yet, to what extent he made a mistake. One of the master craftsmen of literature, not merely of his own time but of any time, Joyce, in *Finnegans Wake*, let technique become an end in itself. Both the life of the artist and his works dissolve into it. The admiration we feel for his unexampled devotion should not blind us to the price he paid for it. He stopped living. Like Proust, he began remembering.

Every artist, in his fashion, faces this dilemma—in the name of life he must choose art—but if he gives up living he runs the risk of losing them both. I believe this crisis is dramatized in *Finnegans Wake*. Joyce was left with no alternative to grinding up his own work and starting over, since nothing of importance, except his work, had happened to him. The consequential events of his life were those of his adolescence and young manhood—in his exile, in his withdrawal from Dublin, he withdrew from the world. Dublin *was* his life, and in *Ulysses* he processed it. *Finnegans Wake* is less an example of the inscrutable ways of genius than an instance of genius having run out of raw material, an artist who found himself with nothing but his own works on his hands. Through technique Joyce endeavored to make it new. I believe this is why it will largely remain impenetrable—not because it seems so verbally opaque, but because it conceals so little of interest. With a little probing the reader senses that he has been there. He has had it. Little new has been added but the difficulty. In solving the puzzle the reader has solved nothing else. It is the same old Dublin, only the life has gone out of it.

The keys to. Given. A way a lone a last a loved a long the riverrun past Eve and Adam's, from swerve of shore to bend of bay, brings us by commodius vicus of recirculation back to Howth Castle and Environs.

As, indeed, it does. We have been there before. If Joyce's effort has a meaning to the writer who will never approach him in technique, it lies in the demonstration that technique is not enough. If devotion to his craft deprives a man of living, it will end in depriving him of art.

II

Literature, as distinct from life, finds it easier to come to terms with such a puzzle as *Finnegans Wake* than with the fact that the author exchanged so much of his life to accomplish it. Joyce took this risk with his eyes open, and accepted the consequences. But we are men as well as artists, and if art is to remain a permissible illusion there must continue to be room in it for life, the very life that is so conspicuously absent from *Finnegans Wake.* Those faded ghosts of Villiers de L'Isle-Adam who let their servants do their living for them are not the answer, on the evidence, to either life or art.

The dilemma is an old one: the relationship between literature and life. In American terms the problem has been academic—life has usually overwhelmed literature, and the artist, haunted by a sense of failure, has been partially consoled by his grip on life. Men seem to be driven into one or the other extremity. On the one hand we have the master craftsman Joyce armed with nothing but silence, exile, and cunning. On the other we have such a figure as D. H. Lawrence, a man of genius, a novelist, and a poet, whose primary concern was not art, but *life,* a man who believed, with a devotion and example equal to that of Joyce, that if life itself could be led to the full art would grow out of it. The purpose of art was to make such life possible. To give up living *for art* would have struck him as a form of madness: one of those tragic delusions, fostered by cant and sophistication, which led men to choose the death in life rather than the life in it. To free men from this deception, to give them life rather than art, made him a poet and a novelist. The gods of Joyce would have struck him as both strange and false.

With characteristic perception, T. S. Eliot was the first to recognize this polarity. In *After Strange Gods* he summed it up in this fashion:

> We are not concerned with the author's *beliefs*, but with the orthodoxy of sensibility and with the sense of tradition, our degree of approaching "that region where dwell the vast hosts of the dead." And Lawrence is for my purposes, an almost perfect example of the heretic. And the most ethically orthodox of the more eminent writers of my time is Mr. Joyce.

This statement exhibits Mr. Eliot's talent for coining the rules, as well as the terms, of the game that he chooses to play. That we are *not* concerned with the author's *beliefs*, but only with the orthodoxy of his sensibility, is an observation, to speak charitably, that throws light only on the man who made it. But the distinction he draws, if not the terms, is central to our discussion. Some writers appear to be orthodox, others heretics. Mr. Eliot's purpose, however, is not merely to throw light on this schism, but by this light to read the heretic out of the church. Lawrence is not merely unorthodox, he is dangerous.

In an essay published more than thirty years ago, entitled "The Shame of the Person," Laura Riding lucidly anticipated Mr. Eliot's position, and the new criticism:

> There results what has come to be called criticism. . . . In the end the literary sense comes to be an authority to write which the

poet is supposed to receive, through criticism, from the age that he lives in. . . . More and more the poet has been made to conform to literature instead of literature to the poet—literature being the name given by criticism to works inspired or obedient to criticism. Less and less is the poet permitted to rely on personal authority. The very word genius, formerly used to denote the power to intensify a sense of life into a sense of literature, has been boycotted by criticism; not so much because it has become gross and meaningless through sentimentality as because professional literature develops a shame of the person, a snobbism against the personal self-reliance which is the nature of genius.

We can see, in Mr. Eliot's attack on Lawrence, how profoundly she grasped the critical trend, whose tone was established, naturally, by Mr. Eliot. In "Tradition and the Individual Talent," the latitude that exists in theory is singularly circumscribed in practice—by talent Mr. Eliot does not mean *genius*, if genius does *not* choose to knuckle under. Mr. Eliot allows that Lawrence had *genius*, but since his talent was unorthodox, his genius was little more than a critical embarrassment. The shame of Lawrence's *person*—the very substance of his genius—could hardly be better expressed. Lawrence also suffered, Mr. Eliot informs us, from "a lack not so much of information as of the critical faculties which education should give, and an incapacity for what we ordinarily call thinking."

At another time, and in another place, this statement

might have served Mr. Eliot as a definition of genius. But Lawrence *suffers* from it. An incapacity for what is ordinarily called thinking did not destroy him, but made him *suspect*. Mr. Eliot's talent for the destructive comment—I mean the lethal, irrelevant comment—is here displayed at its most masterly. It is the donnish form of "A Genius, but—" of Richard Aldington. At the thought of Lawrence a kind of panic seems to rock Mr. Eliot's mind. What begins as criticism slips imperceptibly into abuse:

The point is that Lawrence started life wholly free from any restriction of tradition or institution, that he had no guidance except the Inner Light, the most untrustworthy and deceitful guide that ever offered itself to wandering humanity. It was peculiarly so of Lawrence, who does not appear to have been gifted with the faculty of self-criticism, except in flashes, even to the extent of worldly shrewdness.

If we look for the source of what is unreasonable in Mr. Eliot's treatment of Lawrence, we shall find it in a review of *Ulysses*, written at the time of its publication:

In using the myth, in manipulating a continuous parallel between contemporaneity and antiquity, Mr. Joyce is pursuing a method which others must pursue after him. . . . It is simply a way of controlling, of ordering, of giving a shape and a significance to the immense panorama of futility and anarchy which is contemporary history. . . . It is, I seriously believe, a step toward making the modern world possible in art.

This is both analysis and prophecy, since Mr. Eliot, as a poet, has continued to give a shape to the immense panorama of futility by manipulating parallels. Both Joyce and Eliot are masters of the collage. The works of both men sometimes contain more of the past than they do of the present—a relevant fact, since it is *in* the past that both men have lived.

But to make the modern world possible in art is not the same, as Lawrence would have insisted, as making life possible in the modern world. The myths that Mr. Eliot is at such pains to parallel are, almost without exception, not acceptable to Lawrence. They were, indeed, the very things that made living his life all but impossible. He chose, both as an artist and as a man, not to manipulate myths but life itself. It is this that stigmatizes him as a dangerous heretic. He was, in fact, anarchy compounded, which may explain, if not justify, the element of panic in Mr. Eliot's attack that leads him into such unwarranted abuse. Lawrence is the pagan bull run amok in the critics' orderly arrangement of myths.

There is no need to let Lawrence speak for himself, since Mr. Eliot's attack has the merit of doing that for him. It is Lawrence's *defects*, indeed, that make him important to us. In this world—the one in which we must live—the strange gods of D. H. Lawrence appear to be less strange than those of Mr. Eliot. It is why—as the critic describes them—these defects have the ring of familiar virtues. Lawrence speaks as a *man*, that is, a living man, a fearless and independent man, who attempted to live very much as he wrote. His independence, his stubborn self-reliance, his passionate distaste for cant and humbug are not merely in the vein but in the very grain of the American mind. It is this grain that shows in the mind and prose of Thoreau:

Be it life or death, we crave only reality. If we are really dying, let us hear the rattle in our throat and feel the cold in the extremities; if we are alive, let us go about our business.

This might have served as an epitaph for Lawrence. It brings us face to face with the paradox that it is Lawrence, the Englishman in exile, who speaks for the brave new world, and Eliot, the American in exile, who speaks for the old. It has been the purpose of this inquiry to explain this paradox, not merely how it came to pass, but that it was inevitable. In the poet from St. Louis we have the classic example, carried to its ultimate conclusion, of the American artist's tendency to withdraw into the past, to withdraw, that is, from America. His knowledge of the past being what it is, Mr. Eliot has been able to withdraw into it deeper than any of his forerunners or contemporaries. Insofar as such a past is useful to us, he speaks for it.

Lawrence speaks—whenever he speaks—with a different voice:

For man, the vast marvel is to be alive. For man, as for flower and beast and bird, the supreme triumph is to be most vividly alive. Whatever the unborn and the dead may know, they cannot know the beauty, the marvel of being alive in the flesh. The dead may look after the afterwards. But the magnificent here and now of life in the flesh is ours, and ours alone, and ours only for a time.

That is a voice in the present. It is the speech of a man alive. It is this voice that recommends his wayward genius to us. It is this man of whom we can say—as Picasso said of Matisse—that he has a sun in his belly. The sun in the belly of Mr. Eliot is a mythic sun. It is a clinker to manipulate: the fire has gone out of it. The man alive in the present is that patient etherized on the table, awaiting burial.

In a statement on the importance of the novel, Lawrence observed that "it can inform and lead into new places the flow of our sympathetic consciousness, and it can lead our sympathy away in recoil from things that are dead."

In this, Henry James, the master of consciousness, would have concurred. It is a question of the death in life, or the life in it. We must deal with both. But we must also exercise a preference. Mr. Eliot speaks for the past— that region where dwell the vast hosts of the dead; Lawrence speaks for the present—that region where dwell the rest of us. In these two men, representative men, irreconcilable attitudes toward life and literature come face to face. Each man, in his fashion, seeks to give a form, a shape of significance, to the immense panorama of futility in which we live. Allowing for the truth in each persuasion, it is Eliot who speaks for what lies behind us, and Lawrence, the heretic, who speaks for the territory ahead.

In his essay on Philip Massinger, T. S. Eliot observes:

He is not, however, the only man of letters who, at the moment when a new view of life is wanted, has looked at life through the eyes of his predecessors, and only at manners through his own.

This seems to me a just and penetrating estimate of Mr. Eliot's role in modern life and letters. It does nothing to diminish his importance, but explains the nature of his persuasion. He speaks for the past, and it is the past that speaks to most of us. The present is a sight on which we turn our backs, and lid our eyes. It will not change its nature through a manipulation of parallels. In the sense that Mr. Eliot is important, D. H. Lawrence is indispensable.

III

Life, raw life, the kind we lead every day, whether it leads us into the past or the future, has the curious property of not seeming real *enough*. We have a need, however illusive, for a life that is more real than life. It lies in the imagination. Fiction would seem to be the way it is processed into reality. If this were not so we should have little excuse for art. Life, raw life, would be more than satisfactory in itself. But it seems to be the nature of man to transform—himself, if possible, and then the world around him—and the technique of this transformation is what we call art. When man fails to transform, he loses consciousness, he stops living.

Like Walt Whitman, we were there, we saw, and we suffered, but *where* we were, *what* we saw, and *how* we suffered are a mystery to us until the imagination has given them form. And yet imagination, both talent and imagination are of little value without conception. They are merely the tools, and it is conception that puts them to use. In the novel it is conceptual power, not style or sensibility, that indicates genius, since only conception responds to the organic pressures of life. The conceptual act is the most organic act of man. It is this that unites him with the processes of nature, with the nature of life. If man is nature self-conscious, as we have reason to believe, art is his expanding consciousness, and the creative act, in the deepest sense, is his expanding universe.

The essential ingredient in any artist—essential to what is conceptual in his talent—is his freedom to describe what he sees, and what he feels: his freedom to realize, like Cézanne, his sensations. Essential to him is his freedom to be after strange gods. It is by their strangeness that he will know them, since he conjured them up. They are, by definition, the gods that beckon him into the territory ahead. The spirit of the place, this American place, as it is revealed in Thoreau, Whitman, Melville, and Twain, is the spirit of men who are after strange gods.

To be after them is the artist's calling: to find and serve them is his proper function. His individual talent, if he has one, will displace an old god with a new one—but the new one will bear an astonishing resemblance to the one it displaced. Tradition, insofar as it is living, lives on in him, and he is powerless to thwart it; but what is dead in tradition, the heavy hand of it, he destroys. In this act of destruction he achieves his freedom as an artist, and what is vital in his art is the tradition that he sustains.

The man who lives in the present—in his own present —lives to that extent in both the past and the future: the man who seeks to live elsewhere, both as an artist and as a man, has deceived himself. This is an old deception. It is one of the crowded provinces of art.

As Lawrence reminds us:

. . . there is another kind of poetry; the poetry of that which is at hand: the immediate present. In the immediate present there is no perfection, no consummation, nothing finished. The strands are all flying, quivering, intermingling into the web, the waters shaking the moon.

The artist might well ask how, in such a spinning world as ours, he is to know that he stands in the *present*. There are no pat answers, but there are clues. Since he must live and have his being in a world of clichés, he will know this new world by their absence. He will know it by the fact that he has not been there before. The true territory ahead is what he must imagine for himself. He will recognize it by its strangeness, the lonely pilgrimage through which he attained it, and through the window of his fiction he will breathe the air of his brave new world. Strange, indeed, will be the gods found to inhabit it.

ONE LAW FOR THE LION

A NOTE ON HEMINGWAY, AUGUST, 1961

But what a book, they both agreed, would be the real story of Hemingway, not those he writes but the confessions of the real Ernest Hemingway.   —Gertrude Stein

Not long ago we saw him, a bearded smiling Falstaff, on the cover of *Life*. On the cover he looked good. A composite image of the man, the artist, and the legend. Inside there were pictures of bulls, bullfighters, good food, good wine, and good companions. There was also writing. How long has it been since the man and the legend have stood up better than the *writing?* Now that the lists are closed (excepting the manuscripts he did not choose to publish) the facts are disturbing. It is thirty years since he published *A Farewell to Arms*. If Hemingway had died at that time the body of his best work would have been behind him. Ahead were five novels, but only two major achievements: *Death in the Afternoon* and *For Whom the Bell Tolls*. There was always craft. Disciplined squads of emotions, disciplined words. But the verdict of Sunday, July 2nd, forces upon us the knowledge that he had long lived with—the best of his work lay far in the past.

233

To the committed artist—the artist of which Hemingway is the symbol—an unproductive imaginative life is less a life than a burden. I do not believe he was deceived by the world-wide clamor and praise of *The Old Man and the Sea*, an expression of the world's goodwill and affection rather than its taste. The homage of the world is complex and destroys as much as it celebrates, in particular the world that he helped to create. More than ten years earlier he had let drop that the *Big* one was in a bank vault in Cuba—this Big one was his ace in the hole. How well it tells us that what he was doing, in his own opinion, was not enough. It is not like a man—a man like Hemingway—to let his *Big* fish trail under water while he stands on the pier, empty-handed, with his arms outstretched. In the fable of the old man and the sea the moral may be more pointed than we imagined— his tormenting self-doubt more justified than we would believe.

With luck, courage, and great talent, a man's life might prove to be of some interest, but seldom as interesting as his death. With death his life is something more than the sum of its parts. The parts of Hemingway are memorable and the world has waited for a verdict. How well he knew the ways of the world! Even the young man from Oak Park would have told us that death joins more than it tears asunder, and that it is harder to kill a legend than a man.

Of the parts of Hemingway, man, writer, and legend, the writer is vulnerable. He tells us—

So far, about morals, I know only that what is moral is what you feel good after and what is immoral is what you feel bad after. . . .

and

I was trying to learn to write, commencing with the simplest things, and one of the simplest things of all and most fundamental is violent death.

After the lessons of writing were over what led him to seek out war, the safari, the calculated risk? Was it for raw material, or is there a hint that he would welcome death—as he did life—on his own terms? The age questions everything, answers nothing, and he gave these unanswered questions their style.

Abstract words such as glory, honor, courage, or hallow were obscene beside the concrete names of villages, the numbers of roads, the names of rivers, the numbers of regiments and the dates.

As the writing fell off, the man and the legend became the major work of fiction. The style that shaped so many others also shaped Ernest Hemingway. His art can be measured in the faces we still see around us, but the fullest measure was visible in his own. We learned from his life, from his art, and since it cannot be helped we now learn from his death—but there is no profit in it. We merely learn how little we can be taught. We cannot be taught courage, how to avoid self-destruction, how to preserve or salvage our talents, but we did possibly learn that a man can die without merely having passed away.

In an interview in 1954 Hemingway talked about his good times with James Joyce: "We would go out to drink and Joyce would fall into a fight. He couldn't even see the man so he'd say: 'Deal with him, Hemingway! Deal with him!'"

We share, with Joyce, the confidence that Hemingway would. It is out of this *feeling* that the man, and the facts, emerge into the legend to which we all contribute. To the Danish journalist Vinding, Joyce had this to say of Hemingway:*

"He's a good writer, Hemingway. He writes as he is. We like him. He's a big powerful peasant, as strong as a buffalo. A sportsman. And ready to live the life he writes about. He would never have written it if his body had not allowed him to live it."

A peasant? The description must have pleased him, and what pleases a man is what shapes him: big, powerful, strong as a buffalo. Is it the man who shapes the legend, or the legend that shapes the man?

At what point did the image of the man take precedence over the books, and the legend precedence over the man? On July 2nd, which image came first to mind? The brooding Viking in the Karsh portrait, the man's man on the safari, the author at his desk, the man who went four rounds with Braddock, or the old man, the big fish, and the sea?

A memorable but characteristic economy dictates these successive fashions. We may be amused, or shocked, but we need not apologize. This too is *style*—as unchanging as *his* style. The personality of Hemingway cannot be isolated from the man who wrote the books, or the man who is the legend—the authority of one resides in the other. He is all of a piece. The personality cult of a mass-cult age may use this image as we use brand labels, but that is our problem before it is his.

*Richard Ellmann: *James Joyce*.

Some thirty years ago Laura Riding made this comment—

More and more the poet has been made to conform to literature instead of literature to the poet—literature being the name given by criticism to works inspired or obedient to criticism. Less and less is the poet permitted to rely on personal authority. The very word genius, formerly used to denote the power to intensify a sense of life into a sense of literature, has been boycotted by criticism; not so much because it has become gross and meaningless through sentimentality as because professional literature develops a shame of the person, a snobbism against the personal self-reliance which is the nature of genius.

There was no shame of the person in Hemingway. Personal self-reliance seems to be both the hallmark of the man and the legend. That is good. But is it what Hemingway had? On the escutcheon of his self-reliance, along with bulls, fish, and other heraldic symbols, are cryptic signs as well as curious blemishes. Battle scars? We have to look at the record.

The most curious example of Hemingway's talent is a novella, *The Torrents of Spring*, a burlesque-parody of the style of Sherwood Anderson. An older man, Anderson had been his friend and benefactor. Why did the young lion, the buffalo, turn on him? In his memoirs Anderson tells us this:

I got a letter from Hemingway. This after he had written and published *The Torrents of Spring*. It was certainly the most self-conscious and probably the most completely patronizing letter ever written.

He spoke of the book as something fatal to me. He had, he said, written it on an impulse, taking only six weeks to do it. It was intended to bring to an end, once and for all, the notion there was any worth in my work. This, he said, was a thing he had hated doing, because of his personal regard for me, and he had done it in the interest of literature. Literature, I was to understand, was bigger than either of us.

An impulse lasting six weeks is something more than an impulse. *The Torrents of Spring* is the second book of a young and already acclaimed writer, whose time and energy might have been more profitably spent. How explain it? Momentary aberrations find their release in letters and café brawls. *The Torrents of Spring* is a sustained, carefully planned, and extremely clever effort of annihilation. On the evidence Hemingway felt compelled to clear the field of the only competition he considered serious. It is not the act, to put it charitably, of a self-reliant man. It is the skillfully tactical ploy of a man who is scared. Not of lions and bulls or buffaloes, but of competitors. He took this shot at Anderson from ambush with serious intent to bring him down. Hemingway the sportsman? This too, apparently, on his own terms.

In "The Snows of Kilimanjaro" we find this comment—

He remembered poor Julian and his romantic awe of them [the rich] and how he had started a story once that began, "The very rich are different from you and me." And how some one had said to Julian, Yes they have more money.

At that moment poor Julian, F. Scott Fitzgerald, was poor indeed. Hemingway's books are ornamented and flawed with witty asides, meant to be lethal, dealing with selected friends and foes. Fitzgerald, his friend, was a stricken, burdened man, with a few years to live. Was *poor Julian* designed to cheer him up? The impartiality with which Hemingway would deal with a friend, as well as a foe, is not one of the symptoms of self-reliance. He is still strafing the field of competitors. On the evidence self-reliance may be part of the man on the safari, and part of the legend, but not a part of the author of *The Torrents of Spring*. In the man there is more than sufficient to support a respectable legend, but we do not need the legend to respect the man—only the superman.

He would be the champ, and by 1932 he was. *Death in the Afternoon* is many things, it contains the best and the worst of the writer, and it finds him at the moment he stands at the summit of his world.

The great thing is to last and get your work done and see and hear and learn and understand; and write when there is something that you know; and not before; and not too damned much after.

Was there a writer alive in whose ears these words did not ring? Perhaps two. Sherwood Anderson and Gertrude Stein. Just a few months later Gertrude Stein issued her own version of old worlds conquered, putting the record, and her readers, straight on many things. One was Ernest Hemingway. Alice B. Toklas tells us:

Hemingway had been formed by the two of them [Stein and Anderson] and they were both a little proud and a little ashamed of the work of their minds. . . . They admitted that Hemingway was yellow, he is, Gertrude Stein insisted, just like the flat-boat men on the Mississippi river described by Mark Twain.

Hemingway yellow? The malice of Stein's attack is obvious, but she did not throw her barbs at random, or merely tip them with venom. The wounded lion did not roar. The buffalo did not paw the ground. Perhaps it was not the injustice of the attack that led Hemingway to ignore it. He knew his adversary was his master at this sort of cape work, and he had been the first to strike a low blow. Without excuse or provocation he had attacked a friend, Sherwood Anderson.

There is evidence that Stein's verbal shrapnel hurt Hemingway more, and stayed with him longer, than that he received on the Italian front. Under the buffalo hide he was both tender and vulnerable. A lasting preference for men of action, rather than words, dates from this verbal mawling—good drinking, good shooting, and good fishing companions. Good writers are out. Such self-reliance is another form of exile—he had the verbal shooting range to *himself*. He was the champ, in competition with *himself*. At this point we remember that shadow-boxing was one of his favorite pastimes. At parties, especially. It was dead men, as he said in *Esquire*, that one had to beat.

Self-parody, in both his life and his art, are the fruits of the last decade. The man who entered the trees across the river never fully emerged from E. B. White's bar across the street. He is all but invisible in the recent pages of *Life*. *The Torrents of Spring*, in which he served notice on his friend, Sherwood Anderson, is as nothing to the notice *The Dangerous Summer* served on Ernest Hemingway, author of *Death in the Afternoon* and other books.

In a letter to Maxwell Perkins he said that he had "not been at all hardboiled since July 8, 1918—on the night of which I discovered that that also was vanity."

In *Men at War*:

. . . I had a bad time until I figured it out that nothing could happen to me that had not happened to all men before me.

In *A Farewell to Arms:*

If people bring so much courage to this world the world has to kill them to break them, so of course it kills them. The world breaks every one and afterward many are strong at the broken places. But those that will not break it kills. It kills the very good and the very gentle and the very brave impartially. If you are none of these you can be sure it will kill you too but there will be no special hurry.

In *Death in the Afternoon*:

There comes a place in the guidebook where you must say do not come back until you have skied, had sexual intercourse, shot quail or grouse, or been to the bullfight so that you will know what we are talking about.

That much we know beyond a doubt. What he was talking about. Life and death, and that dance he would describe as grace under pressure. But as for the story, there is one and one only that he would tell us. Nature is good, man is a mess, but Nature will prevail. "We'll all be gone before it's changed too much and if no deluge comes when we are gone it still will rain in summer in the north and hawks will nest in the Cathedral at Santiago and in La Granja. . . . it makes no difference if the fountains play or not."

The "Big Two-Hearted River" that rises in Michigan flows, like the Liffey, around the world. In it he dips his line, and hauls out the changeless immortal trout.

Holding him near the tail, hard to hold, alive, in his hand, he whacked him against the log. The trout quivered, rigid. Nick laid him on the log in the shade and broke the neck of the other fish the same way. He laid them side by side on the log. They were fine trout.

In Spain—

They were all about the same size. I laid them out, side by side, all their heads pointing the same way, and looked at them. They were beautifully colored and firm and hard from the cold water. . . . I took the trout ashore, washed them in the cold, smoothly heavy water above the dam, and then picked some ferns and packed them all in a bag, three trout on a layer of ferns, then another layer of ferns, then three more trout, and then covered them with ferns. They looked nice in the ferns, and now the bag was bulky, and I put it in the shade of the tree.

We have Harold Loeb's testimony that these fish were never caught. Not in Spain. No, they are Hemingway's fish, as unchanging as those of Braque. In Italy—

In the bed of the river there were pebbles and boulders, dry and white in the sun, and the water was clear and swiftly moving and blue in the channels.

But no fish. No, the next fish would be the Big one, and come from the sea. The only Hemingway fish that might be said to have got away.

This is refinement, not repetition. A testing of the blade on the chosen material, as a bullfighter tests his capework on the bull. On this material the blade seldom loses its edge. In time, understandably, the materials are chosen to suit the blade. It becomes the function of the style, not the author, to choose the scene, select the cast, and speak the appropriate words. The simplicity lies in the style, not in the material. The Spanish language is used as a simplifying agent where the situation is often complex. Hemingway knew as well as his friend Fitzgerald that "the very rich are different"—very different indeed, but such a fact did not suit the dictates of the Hemingway style. Complicated types enter this world only to lose their complications. Man must appear simple so that Nature will emerge complex. The restoration of NATURE, writ large, a paradise lost, would seem to be the passion behind Hemingway's reduction of man: the raw material he was able to supply himself. But whether Nature likes it or not, Man too is a piece of Nature, and it is why his disillusion is so often grained with hope.

We are a young nation, but premature loss of creative power is already an old American custom. The exceptions have been among the exiles, such as Eliot and Henry James. Foreign air helped, but did not do as much for Hemingway. The destructive agent was of his own invention—an inflexible style. We see it in the man, in the legend, as well as in the books. Several years ago, in "The Function of Style" (pp. 136–141, above), I made my peace with this style in these terms:

When the young man Hemingway came to the edge of the clearing, when he saw what man had left in the place of nature, he found it something more than an unpleasant shock. He found it unacceptable. In that judgment he has never wavered. It is expressed with finality in his exile. In this feeling, and in his exile, he is not alone, but being an artist he has been able to give his judgment a singular permanence. As the style of Faulkner grew out of his rage—out of the impotence of his rage—the style of Hemingway grew out of the depth and nuance of his disenchantment. Only a man who had believed, with a child's purity of faith, in some haunting dream of life, in its vistas of promise, is capable of forging his disillusion into a work of art. It is love of life that Hemingway's judgment of life reveals. Between the lines of his prose, between the passage and the reader, there is often that far sound of running water, a pine-scented breeze that blows from a cleaner and finer world. It is this air that makes the sight of so many corpses bearable. Invariably it is there—a higher order than the one we see before us in operation—as if the legend of the past were stamped, like a signature, on his brow. We have never had a more resolute moralist. A dream of the good life haunts the scene of all the bad life he so memorably observes, and when under his spell it is the dream of the good life that we possess. For such an artist, should there be anything but praise? Could there be anything conceivably impotent about such a style? It is when we come to brood on his consistency—on the man who does not change, or seem aware of it—that we see that the author, as well as the reader, has been under a spell, the same spell—the spell of a style. The consistency lies in what the style will permit him to think, to feel, and to say.

. . . This style—like the clear water that flows at the heart of all of his fiction—sounds the note of enchantment to the very disenchantment it anticipates. The reader grasps, immediately, that this man is not so tough as he looks. Quite the contrary, he looks and sounds so tough because his heart is so soft. Behind the armor of his prose, the shell of his exile, lurks our old friend Huck Finn, American dreamer, the clean-cut boy who just wishes Aunt Sally would leave him alone, who wants nothing more, nor less, than a clearing of his own in the wilderness. The dream itself he left unchanged, he merely moved to a smaller river, but he brought to it a style that revealed the dream to itself.

. . . In the interests of this style things remain as they are, they do not change. It is a lens of the finest precision; it records, accurately, the author's field of vision, but the price of the performance is that the *field* must remain the same. Time—in the sense of development—must stand still. The timeless quality of the Hemingway snapshot is truly timeless—growth and change have been removed. The illusion of things as they are is raised to a point that has seldom been equaled; a frieze-like sense of permanence enshrines the Big Two-Hearted River and its world-wide tributaries. . . . Good fish and running water serve him as the means of coming to terms with life.

With such a writer, appraisal and reappraisal never end. With his death, the man—and with the man, the writing—grow more complex. He is many men, and only a few would fit into the books the style dictated. That fellow was self-reliant, self-assured, and in spite of his disclaimer, a pretty tough hombre. We shall not soon forget how he looked, and never how he wrote. But it is little wonder, now the lists are closed, that he did not write that book Gertrude Stein suggested: the Confessions of Ernest Hemingway. Strange, indeed, that he did not write it—as he did not write the Big one looming on the horizon—because the function of the style made it impossible. It called for a simpler fellow than Ernest Hemingway actually was. We must come to terms with this composite image for ourselves. On one point, however, there is no question, we know a piece of the continent has fallen, and there is no need to ask for whom it is the bell tolls.